IN MOTION, AT REST

IN MOTION, AT REST
THE EVENT OF THE ATHLETIC BODY

GRANT FARRED

UNIVERSITY OF MINNESOTA PRESS
Minneapolis · London

The University of Minnesota Press gratefully acknowledges financial support from the College of Arts and Sciences at Cornell University for the publication of this book.

An earlier version of chapter 1 was published in "The Event of the Black Body at Rest: Mêlée in Motown," *Cultural Critique* 66 (Spring 2007): 58–77. An earlier version of chapter 3 was published in "Zinedine Zidane and the Event of the Secret," *Chimurenga* 10 (December 2006): 224–30.

Published by the University of Minnesota Press
111 Third Avenue South, Suite 290
Minneapolis, MN 55401-2520
http://www.upress.umn.edu

Library of Congress Cataloging-in-Publication Data

Farred, Grant.
In motion, at rest : the event of the athletic body / Grant Farred.
    Includes bibliographical references and index.
    ISBN 978-0-8166-5023-1 (hc : alk. paper)
    ISBN 978-0-8166-5024-8 (pb : alk. paper)
    1. Sports—Philosophy. 2. Events (Philosophy). 3. Human body (Philosophy). 4. World Peace, Metta, 1979– . 5. Cantona, Éric, 1966– . 6. Zidane, Zinédine, 1972– . 7. Badiou, Alain. 8. Deleuze, Gilles, 1925–1995. 9. Derrida, Jacques. I. Title.
    GV706.F37 2014
    796.01—dc23

                        2013028362

Printed in the United States of America on acid-free paper

The University of Minnesota is an equal-opportunity educator and employer.

20 19 18 17 16 15 14   10 9 8 7 6 5 4 3 2 1

This book is dedicated to my grandparents,
Winnifred and Thomas Fisher.
You gave so much.

CONTENTS

SPORT AND THE EVENT

Both invent *and* bring up to date, inaugurate
and reveal, cause to come about *and* to bring
up to the light *at the same time, there where
they were already there without being there.*
JACQUES DERRIDA, *SPECTERS OF MARX*

Invention not of the event but through the event.
JACQUES DERRIDA, *ROGUES: TWO ESSAYS ON REASON*

The event is sui generis. It stands alone and it exists on its own
terms. We know the event because, in our thinking, in our memory of what happened, it stands as *that* moment. The event is that
precise and unexpected instant that we did not—could not—see
coming; the event transforms entirely a humdrum, or even a crucial, encounter into an historic occurrence. It is only the event
that can, through disrupting the routine, make what is everyday
and unremarkable, be that the annual political rally, the run-of-
the-mill sports contest, the regular social gathering, memorable.

The force of the event resides in its ability to mark itself off
from all the other moments that came before and after. Because of
the event, every moment before and after it must be thought again.
Nonetheless, the event can render all other moments insignificant
or incidental, however much the event sometimes depends on the
incidental to bring it into itself; that is because the event alone
has the power to unexpectedly transform the insignificant into
something of consequence.

And yet, as *In Motion, At Rest: The Event of the Athletic Body*
shows, the event is insufficient in itself. *In Motion*, which traces

1

the events of Ron Artest (basketball), Eric Cantona, and Zinedine Zidane (both football[1]), makes clear that the event cannot be understood except on its own specific terms. In his discussion of the event in relation to love, Alain Badiou, an important contemporary theorist of the event, offers some illumination in this regard. The event "remains quite opaque," Badiou insists, until it "finds reality in its multiple resonances within the real world."[2] To make the event, if not transparent, then markedly less opaque, *In Motion* seeks to identify the "multiple resonances"—the key concepts—as it refers specifically to Artest, Cantona, and Zidane. Prominent among these concepts are the particular idiom of sport, the rareness of the event, the intensity of the event, and the figure of the rogue, although these are, of course, not the only concepts in play. In thinking the event in sport, *In Motion* shows how it is that sport articulates these concepts, variously combined in each of the three events, in a unique way.

In sport, the maxim goes, anything can happen—but this is equally true of, say, politics or global finance. Following this logic, the event, which is always unexpected, is a concept lodged at the core of sport. And yet, in sport, the event is always anticipated. The logic that governs sport is, of course, unpredictability itself: who knows what the game will yield? This logic makes intensely evident the institutionalization of the unpredictable: the event is, a priori, inscribed into sport. But, anticipated though the event might be, the event in sport must always be thought of as more than an interruption of the game as it is going along. (However much sport understands itself as a sociopolitical practice that is "sovereign" to itself, it is not; sport is in no way autonomous.) The event might be anticipated, but it is never knowable in advance, nor can it be fully known in its aftermath. The resonances of the sport's event might, indeed, not be so much multiple as infinite—infinitely unknowable.

The sport's event is that interruption that is capable of producing an irruption: the radical disruption of a sport's encounter that is dispersed into the world, that radical disruption that violently invades the world. The irruption assumes an especial form: that idiom that is particular to sport. In Artest's case, it is the flagrant foul that leads to him (and some of his teammates) "invading" the stands; for his part, it is Cantona's expulsion from a game that leads to him violently attacking a fan in the stands. The effect of the sport's event is that it disrupts both sport and the world beyond it with an intensity that the world could not have imagined. The sport's event cannot be contained to sport, and yet it renders the event inimitable: it presents the event to the world in a form that nothing else can. To invoke Badiou, substituting "sport" for his "art," "sport is what, at the level of thought, does complete justice to events."[3] Out of *In Motion*'s thinking of sport, an entirely new structure of the event emerges. This new structure is made possible by the sport's event, and the sport's event alone.

The sport's event makes clear that part of the event's singularity derives not only from its fidelity to its idiom but from our struggle to know it as an event. It makes clear that the event can only be known if it is properly approached: as a political difficulty. To know the event, it must be distinguished from the familiar. The sport's event has no place in the discourse of the routine—those occurrences in sport, improperly known as "events," that follow the sport's calendar. These occurrences, such as the Super Bowl or the Wimbledon tennis championship, the Masters (golf) or the English Football Association (FA) Cup Final, are presented, unfailingly, with the promise of the spectacular or the dramatic. We are familiar with the discourse, "This will be an event to remember." "What an event it was!" "This will be an event like no other." For the purpose of distinguishing the Super Bowl or Wimbledon from the event (Artest; Zidane), *In Motion* names the former the *pseudo-event*.

Wimbledon or the Super Bowl are pseudo-events labeled "events" because they represent the highlight of, respectively, the annual tennis or American football calendar. (Grammatically phrased, *In Motion* distinguishes between the pseudo-event, rendered here as the "sports event," and the apostrophized "sport's event," which represents the philosophical thinking of the event in relation to sport. Similarly, "sport's time" marks the philosophical ways in which *In Motion* sees the relationship between time and sport, often, of course, in relation to the event.) More to the point, these are colloquially known as "events" because they are marketed as "events"—a great many resources are dedicated to maintaining the status of these annual affairs as "events." We know, however, that what distinguishes the event from the pseudo-event is that the former is neither predictable nor routine; Wimbledon, the Super Bowl, the Masters, these are all predictable, the label "event" mere hyperbole. The event is not the pseudo-event in that the event constitutes precisely that moment in sport that disrupts, often violently, the routine; the effect of the (sport's) event is that it effects everything. The event is the sworn enemy of routine—of the predictability of the calendar—because even though the event, as concept, can be anticipated (it stands at the core of all sport's logic), the event itself cannot be.

The event cannot be penciled in on the year's sports calendar as if it were simply another, albeit more grandiose, version of a game on the season's schedule. Of course, the event may coincide with the pseudo-event. Wimbledon may indeed host a moment of genuine transformation, as the Super Bowl might bear witness to the irruption of violence. That, however, is not expected; in fact, the marketing of the Super Bowl as an "event" turns precisely on foreclosing the prospect of such an irruption of violence. Were the FA Cup to host a radical disruption that made of the pseudo-event an event, it would be entirely coincidental. The event cannot be scheduled. However, the logic of sport is such that within the pseudo-event, there is always the possibility of the event. In sport the event is always, to some extent or other, inevitable. There is a certain paradox to this, a paradox that reveals the force of the event. Sport is a sociopolitical practice that constantly represents itself as an "event." And yet when the event does happen, it not only completely destroys the veneer that is the pseudo-event, it shows sport to be entirely incapable of producing a language of and for the event. The event marks the limits of the idiom of sport and, as Badiou and Martin Heidegger might in their different ways suggest, the beginning of thought—thought that must begin with the event so that it can do "justice" (Badiou) to the event.

THE THREE EVENTS

The opening chapter of *In Motion* turns on the event of Ron Artest when he was playing in the National Basketball Association (NBA) for the Indiana Pacers (he's since become, improbably, "Metta World Peace," of the Los Angeles Lakers; in July 2013, he joined his hometown team, the New York Knicks); the second chapter on Eric Cantona, a French footballer then playing in the English Premier League for Manchester United; and the last chapter on Zinedine Zidane, the French national captain playing in the final game of his career in, of all momentous things, the 2006 World Cup final.

In November 2004, during the waning moments of an NBA game between the Pacers and the hometown Detroit Pistons, Artest instigated a series of actions. There was an altercation with Ben Wallace of the Pistons after Artest had committed a flagrant foul, and then there were scuffles with other players (in which Artest was quickly joined by teammates Stephen Jackson and Jermaine O'Neal). There was Artest, seemingly in the midst of all the mayhem, lying supine on the scorer's table; Detroit Piston fans threw beer on him, as a result of which Artest vaulted into the stands to attack the offending spectators. A huge fallout ensued. The NBA imposed historically severe punishments on Artest, fining him an unprecedented amount and suspending him for a record time. His teammates, too, were fined and suspended, but no other penalty came close to Artest's.

In January 1995, Cantona, playing for Manchester United against Crystal Palace, tired of having to endure harsh physical punishment by his opponents on the field and ethnic invective from the stands, took especial exception to one fan's attack on his Frenchness. After being dismissed from the game ("red carded," in football parlance), and finally impatient with this fan's disparaging remarks about him and his native country, Cantona stormed the stands and kung fu kicked the offending fan. Like Artest, Cantona was heavily punished.

In Berlin in 2006, Zidane head butted an opponent, Marco Materazzi, after an exchange of words between the two players. Zidane, who retired after this game, left football in a most singular fashion. No player has ever retired after, in full view of the world (if not the camera in that moment), executing a *coup de boule*—leaving the game because of what you did with your head—maybe, even, for Zidane, leaving the game with your head held high.

In Motion recognizes that the sport's event is, as Derrida suggests, "unique, unforeseeable, without horizon, un-masterable by any ipseity or any conventional and thus consensual performativity."[4] The event, in sport or elsewhere, is exceptional because of its ability to open things up, to take things in unexpected directions. And yet, what *In Motion* reveals tends toward the obvious. The events of Artest, Cantona, and Zidane show what is "already there"—what is self-evident—in the sport's event: the sport's event is mobile, and so all belonging (to the sport's event) is transient. The event of *In Motion* belongs to the singular, physical idiom of football and basketball, but it opens up, opens out of the sport's event, beyond sport. It opens out precisely because of the ways in which the sport's event, as Derrida argues, "invents and brings up to date, inaugurates and reveals," through the particularity of its idiom, through the ways in which its idiom operates; *In Motion* mobilizes the athletic body for a more profound interrogation of the event so that the event of *In Motion* belongs only initially, and then only provisionally, to sport. The event of *In Motion* begins with sport, but it is by no means exhausted there. (Every idiom possesses—in making the event it produces—its own poetic. Every idiom has its own poetry, its own—vernacular—immemorable mode of expression.

Every idiom, in its making, in its being made, produces a singular mode of poetry. There is thus something poetic about each one of *In Motion*'s figures; from, as we will see, Eric Cantona's penchant for gnomic phrasing to Ron Artest's historically resonant stillness—what is sometimes, as evidence of the event's poetry, designated as his at restness.)

In Motion proposes, following Derrida, a catalytic articulation of the event, an understanding of the event that begins in and proceeds through motion. It is only possible to truly think the event if the event is approached, a priori, as unrecognizable—"unique, unforeseeable, un-masterable"—and salient. The "pure eventfulness" of what takes place, what is not yet known as the event, apprehends us so that it sets in motion a thinking "without horizon" about what has taken place.[5] Full understanding of the event is (always) to come, but we begin with the recognition that "something" has happened, "something"—of note—has taken place, the force of which leads to a thinking beyond "ipseity or any conventional and thus consensual performativity." This thinking of the event demands that we set aside that which is presumed to be known about the event—that which conforms to the "conventions" of the event. Instead, *In Motion* seeks to understand how what is "unique" and entirely unanticipated, the sport's event, shifts, challenges, reconceives, and repurposes our thinking of the event. *In Motion*'s sport's event makes it possible to not just think the event again but to think the sport's event as the horizon of the event's un-thought. *In Motion* thinks those elements of the event that have never been brought properly into view, have never been considered before; *In Motion* does the sport's event justice by thinking it, in the final instance, as an event before all else.

To this end, the event must be approached, firstly, instrumentally, if, that is, we understand "instrumentally" in the best possible sense: from the position of ἐφευρίσκω *(epheurisko/heuriskein)* or *heuresis,* as the creation of something new, or, at least, different—to think the sport's event as the "invention of the event," to think how the event makes itself. In the logic of *In Motion,* however, *heuresis* is made secondary to invention through praxis (πρᾶξις). It is only possible to come to the invention of the sport's event through an explication of the praxis of the event. In this instance, *praxis* means the idiom of sport: the particular language that is permissible, or not (in their own way, the chapters on Cantona and Zidane—but especially the latter—turn precisely on what can be said, or not, within the context of a football game, even one so prestigious as the World Cup final), the practices of sport, the ways in which violence is crucial to those practices, the ways in which race and ethnicity articulate themselves, the ways in which bodies are allowed to move, the relationship between the athlete's space and that of the spectator (Cantona), what happens when those spaces (and temporalities) come into conflict, and so on. The sport's event invents the event through and in the idiom of the event. The force of the idiom makes it possible to understand why Derrida is unyielding: "invention *not* of the event but through the event" (emphasis added). We can only understand the event *through* the event. What is made is made *through* the event (no other making is possible), leading us to praxis (πρᾶξις), the idiom, because that is the only way in which to understand how the process of the event unfolds. To understand the event, it is absolutely necessary to focus first on the *how* of how the event is made: to restore, through the idiom, the particular effect of what it means to go *through* the event. *In Motion* takes the measure of how much it takes, without being able to fully account for it, to invent (ἐφευρίσκω) the sport's event.

THE IDIOM

To grasp the sport's event, it is imperative to think the practice—football, basketball, and all that is gathered into it—of the sport's event.[6] It is imperative to think, that is, the "unique, unforeseeable, without horizon, un-masterable ipseity" of the sport's event: to open out onto, without expectation and yet full of anticipation, the utterly ungraspable ipseity of a sport, to open out onto the irrepressible selfness of a game of football or basketball in the full knowledge that anything might happen. Understanding the event begins from the recognition that what is "already there" can only be apprehended, and then, of course, only provisionally, in the moment of its unfolding, in the moment in which what is "already there" makes itself unutterably palpable and unarguably present. This is the moment when we know, as Derrida would rightly insist (allowing for the recalibrated phrasing), the "pure eventfulness of the sport's event." Confronting the intense accumulation of possibilities located in the events of Artest, Cantona, and Zidane is what it means for *In Motion* to come to terms with what is "purely eventful," what happens in, what happens because of, the sport's event. Precisely, what kind of thinking about the event does the "pure eventfulness" of the sport's event provoke? At the very least, as *In Motion* shows, the "pure eventfulness" of the sport's event gives rise to an intricate philosophical interplay: the interplay among athletic bodies in motion, athletic bodies at rest, and the recognition of the relationship between the permeability and particularity of the idiom. What is said on a football field, for example, achieves a particular intensity there, but it is as likely to derive from the kind of things footballers say routinely to teammates (on the training ground, in the locker room, in a pub, over meals) and opponents (on the field, in the heat of battle) as it is to draw from more widely shared speech. What is permissible on the football field may, of course, constitute a transgression or give offense off of it, or not. Banter about race, sexual orientation, and ethnic background could contribute toward team bonding or secure personal friendships; it could as easily become the cause of a grievance. *In Motion* thinks the idiom in terms of its im-mobility. Out of its idiom, the sport's event produces a thinking about the event that shuttles, sometimes awkwardly, sometimes through a determination to think the "out onto" to its very limit (a limit we cannot possibly know), between the singularity of the sport's event and its difficult relationship to the event as such.

It is because this interplay is unmasterable that *In Motion,* simultaneously, offers sport as a template for thinking every other event and is hesitant about—almost draws back from—(advancing) that claim. To state the terms of this paradox, though *In Motion* does not propose the event in sport as the exception that proves the rule—it is by no means a "special" state of exception— it nevertheless reveals what is particular about the sport's event. Though the sport's event is not the exception as such, sport is nonetheless—and this is where its particularity enunciates itself— the most intense version of a logic that is smeared everywhere across the spectrum. The sport's event makes the logic of the event, its "characteristic" eventfulness (what is characteristic, or "pure," about its eventfulness), visible in a fashion that no other articulation of the event can.

In the sport's event of Artest, Cantona, and Zidane, it is simply easier to "see"—to observe, to witness, to write, to think—that logic in its most intensely panoptic or synoptic disciplinary forms. In the event on the football field or the basketball court, the logic of the event is more "visible." It is, however, more visible only because the possibility of disorder is widely understood to be inherent to and constitutive of sport. This is where we encounter the "unmasterable ipseity" out of which the disorder of possibility emerges, a disorder that is, of course, eminently capable of imposing its own order, of imposing itself as a new structure of and for order. In this way, the event is expected in sport because disorder is always constitutively possible; the event is native to sport, it is nothing less than the very selfness of sport. Above all else, sport is the very incarnation of the event to come. The inauguration and revelation of the event is, so to speak, immanently present in any situation.

However, again by this same logic, the event is also entirely unexpected. After all, there is no reason (and yet every reason, of course) that the flagrant foul should become the event. Why should one invective, or a string of them (but always singular in their articulation), produce the *coup de boule,* while another, similarly constructed series of expletives aimed at the Other, uttered in the same tone (or greater vitriol, even), leads to nothing? The sport's event only comes into itself on its own idiomatic terms, in its unknowable time, a time common to or shared by all history, and yet not. In the meanwhile, there is nothing—which is to say that it is everything—but anticipation for the event. The effect of disorder, which owes a great deal to difference (the event is particular and is absolutely felicitous to the moment and to the idiomatic condition of its making), is that it prepares one for, at any moment, the possibility of deformation. Sport is always, whether or not we acknowledge it, on the verge—on the precipice—of a radical rupture of the "wholeness," the easily impeachable logic of order, that sport needs just to exist. Sport is, as it were, inordinately vulnerable to deformation for no reason other than autoimmunity: it is made out of deformation. What would sport be without the constant possibility—it would not be entirely improper to label it "the threat"—of something entirely unexpected (violence, brilliance, transgression)? The game deformed, or, at the very least, transformed, by the very elements that constitute it? To simply play the game, this logic—that nothing will interrupt it, that the game can be played, without incident, from beginning to end—is constitutive. As much as it is, needless to say, constitutive of sport's autoimmunity, the logic of disorder is built into, from the very beginning, the desire for order, that desire that announces itself as the "rules of the game."

Once the game has been de-formed in the guise of, say, the interruption of the contest, the conditions have been created to produce the event out of that unexpected deformation. The possibility of disorder (or the impossibility of uninterrupted order) is built into the logic of the game from the very beginning. The possibility of disorder is always inherently present. Deformity or impossibility, that is, the event, is not rare; it is everywhere. It is omnipresent, like the rogue, who, in *In Motion,* figures as the unexceptional exception, all around us.

The effect of the rogue is on how, in relation to sport, the law knows itself as, before all else, vulnerable. The law is vulnerable before everything that the game might produce, vulnerable to everything that might emerge out of the game. Sport is, by its very nature and logic, uniquely unmasterable: sport does not, cannot, know what will be released out of its ipseity—out of its disorderly selfness. But sport does know, and it prides itself on this, that it cannot eliminate unforseeability from sport any more than it can exile the rogue from its ranks. In fact, sport has always had a peculiar love and admiration for the rogue, despite the threat that this figure poses.

INTENSITY AND THE IDIOM

The events of Artest, Cantona, and Zidane show how thinking the event through sport—through the event made by sport—is possible only if such an event alternately establishes and disavows its singularity. These sports events show how what Cantona or Zidane initiates is, firstly, an event. What happens in sport utterly transforms how we understand what took place between two athletes or between athletes and fans and produces an understanding of race or ethnicity, movement or stillness, wrought by sport that far exceeds sport. The event of Cantona or Zidane is made by and in its own idiom, an idiom that begins in a very particular way: with intensity. The idiom is always an intensification of the ways in which the language of race, ethnicity, or xenophobia is expressed in a sport's contest. The intensity of the idiom is such that it is almost impossible to imagine it being articulated in this fashion outside of the basketball arena or the football match, an articulation that commands its own currency in a sporting encounter. The idiom of the event is bound to intensity, to the intensity that is particular to the event. That is, the intensity of the event cannot be disarticulated from, cannot be understood without, the specific idiom of the event.

To continue this paradoxical line of thought, as the Zidane chapter makes apparent, the logic of the event is that the event is

secret—open, everywhere (presumed to be) known—but somehow still obscure, unknowable, elusive, *voyou*-ish. The event
reverberates in part, as *In Motion* shows, because of its scarcity,
but much more so because of its deformed, impossible ubiquity.
It is the peculiar intensity of sport that leads to the event's reverberation. It follows, of course, that the greater the intensity of the
event, the more pronounced and ubiquitous the reverberations.
The possibility for the event, then, is ubiquitous, which means
that the event is always expected to happen and yet takes everyone
entirely by surprise when it announces itself, to say nothing of the
incomprehension that attends to its speaking itself idiomatically.

There is a perfectly plausible logic at work here. The event
can be known while remaining unknowable because the only
truth to the event is its own idiom, which remains hidden from
the event (itself) until the idiom makes possible the event. The
sport's event, then, compels a thinking of difference; Zidane, for
example, is distinguished from his 2006 World Cup final adver-
sary, Marco Materazzi, because they represent different orders of
the *voyou*. The event is difference, but not only difference. And
yet, like the event, *différance* is everywhere.[7] But what the sport's
event reveals is that *différance* may be more intensely present—
"visible," performed, constative—in the sport's event than it is
anywhere else, more intensely present in the sport's event than
in, say, a novel or a poem.

The event is intense in its particularity, uncannily unto itself.
And, it must said, necessarily so. What matters is that the event
is rendered in an idiom that is unique to the event out of which
it arises. The event is rendered in an idiom that is sometimes
overdetermined by the intensity of the moment. That idiom is,
for the event of Zidane, specific to the intensity of the football
field on which the World Cup final is being played, or, for Artest
and Cantona, it is the intensity as it is produced by the time and
space of the stadium. And always, of course, *In Motion* recognizes
that idiom is particular to the assembly of athletes (and fans, of
course, in the case of Artest and Cantona) out of which the event

arises—Artest and Wallace, Cantona and the Crystal Palace defender Richard Shaw.

There is, of course, a trace of that idiom rendered elsewhere. The trace is both surplus to and constitutive of the event. There are, however, different levels of intensity of that event that reverberate across various media spectra, specters of the event register variously in sites outside of, and in addition to, of course, the event itself. There are different levels of intensity at work on the field, in the stands, on television, on the Internet—that is, all the various social media that constitute new technologies.

The force of the idiom, its intensity, derives from its unexpected capacity to draw the history of, say, racism or xenophobia into the articulation, thereby transforming, with a rare speed and intensity, the initial articulation, locating that articulation at once firmly within the sports contest—making it particular to its context—and then disseminating it into the wider world. Because of the event, "after" the event (because one of the key features of the event is that it resists any final speaking, "closure"), what Zidane said, or did not say, cannot be contained to the football field. His silence belongs, because of the event, to the world—not simply to the pseudo-event of the World Cup but to the event that he made for the world. It belongs to, we might say, history. The event, in making itself historic, because of its idiom, is responsible for the very stuff of history; derived from the event is the rhetorical texture, the verbal grit, a certain viscerality, a palpability, of what happened—this is, we are again reminded, the "pure eventfulness of the event." The event lives most fully in its idiom. The kung fu kick, the *coup de boule*: the historicity of the event resides in its power to name itself, always returning us to the name in question, to the questioning of the name. The event knows itself, first, through its own naming. This idiomatic concatenation, names/self-naming, unexpected gathering, movement, stillness, silence, wrenching history from itself, is what makes the event. Out of these materials, the sport's event structures itself.

It is only through its particular idiom, race or ethnicity, movement or stasis, and its capacity to Gather other Situations (say, the history of racism in the United States or historic Anglo-French antipathy) toward or into it, that the transgression in the basketball arena, in the football stands and on the football field, always marked by a singular intensity, can become an event. Because of the idiomatic intensity of the event, the athlete brings the event "up to date"—makes the sports event a matter that can only be properly understood in the terms of contemporary philosophy, as a thinking of the event that elucidates the event for contemporary philosophy. The event of Artest or Zidane renews, reinvigorates, and intensifies the event, offering itself for thinking as if it has not yet been thought. *In Motion*'s thinking the sport's event is in itself, of course, a critique of why the event has not been thought in relation to sport.

Such is the nature of double duty that the event demands that "inauguration," of the "new structure of the event," and "revelation," showing the event what it is lacking, how it needs to think itself in the wake of the revelation, in the wake of what the sport's event "brings up to the light," the interrogative, conceptual light that the sport's event holds up to the event itself, take place "at the same time." The key Situation or transformative incident in sport belongs, then, a priori, to the thinking of the event, thinking the event under the condition, à la St. Paul, of an inaugural violence.

It is only possible to think, a difficult proposition, the sport's event in its singularity if it is thought, first and last, as the event. This is because the sport's event brings to light nothing less than that act and its variegated, infinitely unpredictable supplement, which belongs properly—that is, its proper philosophical place— to the event. The new structure of the sport's event is made out of the disorder of possibility. The new structure of the event turns on unpredictability (will the transgression "progress" into an event or will it remain a transgression?), the act of transgression itself, rareness, violence, all of it centered around an idiomatic core: the ways in which race, ethnicity, the history of race and ethnicity, and the secret of the *voyou* stipulate to those disordered forces that can be gathered into it. It is through the idiom that the disorder of possibility disperses the event into the world; it is through the idiom that the event is disseminated into the world and makes its claim on the world.

In Motion returns again and again, in all three events, to the centrality—the essentiality or ontology—of the idiom. The event begins in the idiom, the event makes itself known through the idiom. *In Motion* is inscribed, from Artest to Cantona to Zidane, in the idiom, it is a writing of the idiom. *In Motion* is a structure of the event signed into being by the idiom; the idiom, particular; the idiom is what makes possible the recognition of other idioms. The idiom is, of course, true to itself. Because of this, the idiom understands that it can only be also true to itself if it is true to all idioms in their singularity—a singular union, this union of singularities.

THE ROGUE

If the United States is, as Derrida argues in *Rogues: Two Essays on Reason,* the supreme *etat voyou* (in significant measure because it will not think its own acts in terms of the relationship between reason and force[8]), then the United States is no different from any other state. It is the very logic of the state (its belief in its own exceptionality, its sovereignty, its "monopoly" on force, if not violence—a fact brought home, of course, with the event of September 11) that makes the state an *etat voyou*. It is for this reason that, much as the state appeals to wholeness or law-abidingness, it can, of course, never function according to that logic.[9] If the United States is a rogue state, then it is exactly like every superstar athlete, from Jack Johnson to Babe Ruth, from Mickey Mantle to Muhammad Ali, from Diego Maradona to Zidane—to say nothing of Artest and Cantona, of course. The logic of the star athlete is *voyou*-ish, as the chapter on Zidane makes clear. So, if the political has no use for either wholeness or the "final interpretation" (and neither, of course, does literature, politics, or history), then what is left for the sport's event is a signal challenge: it must reveal that what is rare is not the event as such. And this can only be achieved by thinking the event against "any conventional and thus consensual performativity," by thinking (for) something other than rareness without completely abandoning rareness. This can only be achieved by thinking (for) something, thinking (for that) something, from rareness itself.

The events of Artest, Cantona, and Zidane demonstrate that what is genuinely rare is a really intense version of the event. (There is, then, a tension steeped in *différance,* an admittedly precarious distinction that marks the event as something "less than" its intensified self. The intensified event is visible in terms of its effect and the particularity of its idiom, the event of Artest, Cantona, and Zidane. The intensified event demands, in St. Paul's terms, nothing less than being violently yanked off a donkey. Without that act of violence, Paul has no way of coming to Jesus-the-Christ, no way of becoming an apostle. There is, obviously, no place for the pseudo-event in this conversation.) Opposing players have words in every game, one could safely say; players are heckled by spectators, to some extent or other, at almost every NBA venue, at every stadium where professional football is played. (And, as every weekend competitor knows, the amateur game is no stranger to such animosities either, without, of course, the requisite skill level.) Clearly, however, not every exchange of verbal hostilities between players ends in a head butt, nor does every malicious remark or xenophobic jibe by a spectator result in the player taking to the stands. *In Motion* shows how it is "through the event" that the event produces "an Artest" or "a Cantona" as much as "an Artest" or "a Cantona" is instrumental to making the event—"invention," as Derrida insists, correctly, "not of the event but through the event": πρᾶξις.

Let us pause here to grasp fully what is at stake by posing a question about the likelihood or frequency of an event. What is more rare, a thinking of the state as *etat voyou* or the French captain head butting his Italian opponent in the World Cup final?

The *etat voyou* is, it would seem, everywhere. Every state is, by one definition or another, a rogue state. The United States, Iran, the Sudan, Cuba, would all, according to one set of precepts or another, qualify, much as we might disagree on the designation. Conversely, we know the *coup de boule* is definitely not ubiquitous. A head butt in a World Cup final is rare, extremely unlikely to happen. The *coup de boule* is defined through its praxis, through how it makes—invents—the event. In addition, the *coup de boule* is known through the rareness of its intensity as well as through the intensity of its idiom—and, of course, the intensity of its reverberations as well as its effects, political and otherwise. The effect of this new structure of the event—in all its idiomatic particularity, because of its idiomatic particularity, its rareness and its intensity—is to distinguish it not from the pseudo-event (which is done easily enough); rather, the effect of this new structure of the event is to distinguish it from the event as we have previously known it. This new structure makes us begin again, this time in search of what is "already there without being already there." What is already there that we have not attended to? What is it that thinking on the event has missed?

A NEW STRUCTURE FOR THE EVENT

Artest, Cantona, and Zidane have given us a new structure of the event. This is a complex structure that derives from scarcity and rareness and yet recognizes that autoimmunity—the disorder that belongs, first and foremost, to the logic of order, the transgression that has the potential to make the event—is not only constitutive of the event but ubiquitously present. The event, like the rogue, is idiomatically itself. The event is its own idiom. The event is everywhere, and yet it remains felicitously singular, recognizable only as itself. Thinking through and against transgression, through rareness, singularity, and ubiquity, through movement, stillness, and *voyou*-ishness, through the idiom and intensity, what *In Motion* clearly demonstrates is the provocation that the sport's event offers. These various elements, in their infinitely varied concatenation, compose the new structure of the event. If the extant structure of the event is understood to arise out of strictly political conditions, *In Motion* proposes a new architecture for the event.

It is a fairly simple structure, composed of various primary poles that allow for movement among themselves. Some poles might have greater salience than others, but the organizing principle is not the primacy of the poles but the philosophical "energy" that they generate—the kinetic energy that instigates movement (of the various elements) between poles, the kinetic energy that can transform the elements in each pole and, in so doing, make possible the transformation of not only an individual pole but the entire structure.

In Motion's poles are the idiom, intensity, movement (action), and stillness (inertia), the last being, arguably, by itself, the most important. Or it could be said to derive its importance from the interplay between movement and subtraction. Each of *In Motion*'s figures, in his own way, understands the importance of abstracting himself from the action. Each understands the importance of being at rest. Artest, Cantona, and Zidane grasp, powerfully, intuitively (here one must speculate), the effect their subtraction will have on the event that they are in the process of making.

In the space between the poles, their constitutive elements mingle and reinforce each other. Some of these elements can be traced to one pole or the other, but this is by no means a proprietary relationship. In this way, some aspects of language, say, the secret, gravitate more toward one pole (intensity), while others, say, xenophobic invective, tend more toward the idiom. For the most part, however, the space between houses a combustible series of exchanges among elements such as language (a thinking that is tuned especially to what is said on and off, say, the football field, always seeking to explicate, no matter the difficulty of this task, why one mode of expression, one term, provokes the event and others, measurably similar, cause no effects whatsoever), culture (an expansive and elastic thinking about social practices—a thinking that stretches across, and links, continents; a thinking for difference, in short), and politics (a thinking that engages political issues, race, ethnicity, immigration, as integral to and constitutive of the event, without ever privileging it).[10]

This structure is at once solidly grounded and fluid. This operates on the basis of the free play of possibility; the event can be made out of any series of concatenations between or among the various elements. Occasionally, other poles might arise, some temporary, others permanent. In Zidane's case, for example, the secret and the *voyou* emerge so strongly as to constitute their own poles, but they are also constitutively vulnerable to being absorbed by other poles. Every event is constructed out of its own poles. It is always from these poles that the event can be said to "flow"; the poles provide the primary structure of the event. The greater the salience of these poles, the greater sport's philosophical clarity.

Consequently, the first task of this new structure is to make thinkable—to illuminate—that which was already there but could only now be made opaque (not in Badiou's sense), properly thinkable, because of the sport's event. *In Motion*'s structure of the sport's event makes it possible to know that which was already there but was not (yet) thought. Because of Artest, Cantona, and Zidane, that which was not known before, is now, because of the sport's event and its particular structure, eminently known. At the very least, the effect of this structural renovation is to provoke a thinking about that which is not (yet) known about either the event or sport.

TO FOLLOW DISORDER

The filiations that disorder enables—facilitates—are only possible in sport because, no matter how the (various) games' practitioners wish to "structure" the game, there is always lurking, in the very next play or the one in which it is least expected, the possibility of a (glorious) disorder. Out of this disordered set of possibilities (why would a player such as Artest choose, when he has never done anything like it before, rest—to lay supine—rather than continuing to battle an opponent? Why would a player such as Cantona go into the stands to attack a fan in one game when he has ignored their xenophobia many times before?), none of which can ever be predicted, the sport's event emerges. The sport's event can only come properly into being, can only come fully into its own, can only discharge its historic responsibility to the event (a responsibility unknown to itself until that very moment), out of disordered possibility.

Thinking the sport's event does not so much return us to the event (although it clearly does that) as it makes us turn away from the event (if only for a brief moment) in order that the event might now be seen in its new—which is also its proper—light. It is for this reason that Derrida makes his final demand, his recognition that is grounded in *Specters of Marx*'s preoccupation with how to "apostrophize" the ghost—how Marcellus, the scholar, might speak to it, how Hamlet might learn to speak to his father the dead king—that is, that language must be crafted, much like the sport's event must craft a new language for the event that can, as it were, be heard by the ghost behind the visor. That language, how it is now necessary to think the event in, from, because of, its "new structure," is girded by Derrida's persistent poetic: it is already here, it must be looked for, because it is here (what St. Paul, or the apostle Donald Harman Akenson insists on recognizing as "Saint Saul," would name "revelation"[11]). It, be that the language that the ghost needs or the new structure of the event, is before us even as it is so tauntingly absent. In Derrida's evocative phrasing, "where they were already there without being there."

It is only possible, in the terms of *In Motion,* to bring about the new structure by pursuing that which is not yet there, by following the disorder to its end (the event), by exhibiting fidelity to the possibility inherent in the disorder so that the event might be made legible, so that the pure eventfulness of what happened is not sacrificed to the logic of transgression—so that the integrity of the disorder, its constitutive event-fulness (the fullness of the event overwhelms the event, brings the event into its eventfulness), can be properly stipulated. The sport's event can demonstrate what is "already there" in the event only because it is not yet part, it does not belong, it cannot but belong, to what is "already here." Only because there is always a danger that the transgression that precipitates and precedes the event and the disorder—the violence of the melee in Motown, the powerful silence of the *voyou* after the *coup de boule*—that follows the event can easily obscure it. The event-fulness of Cantona's charge into the stands makes it evident that what is "already here" is not adequate to what must be thought (or "brought") here. And what must be thought here is nothing other than the unflinching logic of the disorder of possibility—in order, of course, that the logic of disorder be understood as the only mode through which, out of which, the event can come into being. It is only through this logic that the event can be known as an event.

It is this force of understanding the possibilities for the event in disorder that is brought to life by the sport's event. The event can only be brought to life by thinking transgression or rareness as that which is "already here"—all too visibly, we might say—but does not allow for the revelation of what should be here. Thinking transgression or rareness per se obscures that which is tantalizingly discernible—it is not, of course, fully delineated, but it can be glimpsed, in outline, sometimes vaguely, sometimes in sharp focus—but has to be extracted, pulled from, as it were, the ghost of the event. It is only possible to apprehend Derrida's "there without being there" by refusing the limits of transgression or rareness. What has to be extracted, to state this baldly, is the way in which the disorder of the event constitutes its own, sui generis order—the very event-fulness of the event depends on this philosophical platform. The idiomatic logic of the event is contained within disorder; that logic is always powerfully "there," present in the possibilities that attend to disorder—the event-fulness of the event is always "present" in the disorder; it is legible as the "pure eventfulness of the event." What *In Motion* demonstrates is how to follow the disorder of possibility to the event. The path to the event lies through, Artest, Cantona, and Zidane make abundantly clear, the disorder of possibility—through the possibility (it might even be possibilities) that can only be discerned in and because of disorder.

In every disorder, as reading after reading of *Hamlet* never fails to remind us, there are ghosts, many possibilities for ghosts to announce themselves, many conjunctures where ghosts might (silently, secretly) take up residence. The presence of ghosts in disorder explains the call issued by *Specters of Marx*—it is the specter, Derrida admits, that calls, that has long called, him to Marx. No account of the event can be complete (or adequate) without the "being there"—the inaugural, revelatory presence—of those who were once only ghosts to the event, an Artest or a Zidane. It is these athletes, and, of course, by no means them alone, who can bring the event up to date. After, that is, they have invented a new structure—made in their own idiom, dispersed from the idiom, disseminated through the idiom—through which the event might be brought to light. Artest, Cantona, and Zidane instantiate the athletic body in motion, at rest, always, simply by its particular "being there," capable of giving an idiomatic shape to the event—a shape such as the event did not know, did not know it could possess, did not know was possible until the possibilities contained within disorder were recognized. The event did not know it could possess it "there," on the football field, on the basketball court; the event did not know that the shape of the event was "already there," did not know it could possess it in so philosophically visible a shape.

RON ARTEST
The Black Body at Rest (Alain Badiou)

A body is called finite because we can always conceive
another which is greater. In the same way, a thought
is limited by another thought. But a body is not
limited by a thought, nor a thought by a body.

SPINOZA, *ETHICS*

During a November 2004 NBA game between the Indiana Pacers
and the Detroit Pistons, a rapid sequence of physical exchanges
culminated in Ron Artest charging into the stands to attack Pistons
fans. With less than a minute left in the game and his Pacers leading handily, Artest, throughout his career one of best defenders
in the NBA, committed a flagrant foul on the Pistons' center, Ben
Wallace. Taking offense at the foul, Wallace shoved Artest—
nothing unusual in an NBA game. What happened after that,
however, was entirely unexpected. Instead of engaging Wallace
or the other Pistons, Artest retreated to the scorer's table. There
he lay, not only supine but still, at rest, an act that was at once
a kind of taunting and, importantly, a subtraction—in Alain
Badiou's terms—from the event. (The refusal to move amounted,
of course, to a substantial addition to the event's intensity.)

In Badiou's thinking, there is a close relationship between his
"subtractive" practice and his insistent advocacy of the multiple.
For Badiou, there is nothing but multiplicity: material events give
birth to multiple possibilities, which explains Badiou's fidelity to
the event; fidelity to the event gives rise to possibility, the possibility, most importantly, of things being otherwise, in a very

specific way—which is why 1848 and 1917 figure so prominently in Badiou's thinking. What Badiou seeks to do is break the bonds of, or subtract from (wrest away with philosophical and political force), a discourse that is too tightly bound to one suture or explanation (one overdetermined attachment, one overcommitted investment) to reconnect it with the multiple. Thus the event is, as it were, opened up, not only to others—other forces, other historical moments—but also to itself. As multiple, the event is released into the possibility of variegated connections. In this instance, the event of Artest is "unbound" from itself and opened into interruption as stasis: the slowing down of movement until the athletic body is at rest, which then sets in motion an entirely new and different set of actions.

Because of this multiplicity, then, Artest's actions can be understood to matter intensely and not to matter at all—in relation to the act of stasis, of course. Artest's actions matter. The flagrant foul, the physical engagement with the fans, and the decision not to act (an action in itself) have consequences, not least of which is conjuring the material force of the event of stasis as refusal—the right to refuse movement, the right to remain at rest in the midst of the very, the every, action that this stillness has instigated and then gathered to itself. However, thinking through stasis enables one to understand the event as interruption: as the irruption of race in the NBA and as the force of the multiple. What the multiple does is destroy the calcified understanding of the event—because of the multiple, the event can never belong to only one suture or another. The year 1917 cannot be posited only as a political event; the event of Ron Artest is subtracted from mere suture to sports discourse and reconnected, as this chapter will show, with the multiple other registers in which this event resonates. Because of the multiple, the event is not only opened up to itself—as its multiple, uncontainable self—but also exceeds itself, in its gathering, to graft Heidegger's concept onto Badiou's practice, as it were. Fidelity to the force of the event because of the ability to make something like "meaning" out of the event of stasis is given only by the event itself, which each time arranges and rearranges the terms of the event (although the event "invents" the terms themselves). Artest's decision to lie supine on the scorer's table is the act of a *voyou* taunting not only his opponents and the Pistons fans but the law itself: Artest takes up the place of officialdom, NBA timekeeping (and scorekeeping, of course), and thus demonstrates, through the situation his transgression has created, the law's inability to keep order. Artest's decision to remain at rest sets the stage for a run-of-the-mill incident—what would have remained a situation—in the NBA to become an event. Race, as we shall see, is already introduced into the event by the prior deployment of the event.

In the United States, when the black body is still, spectacularly still, of its own volition, it performs at least two political functions. First, the self-immobilized body draws attention to itself (a *voyou*-ish provocation), almost invariably disrupting everything around it, and second, the spectacularly still black body dis-connects—less through chance than through the force of the historical multiple—to other historically self-immobilized black bodies. The black body at rest can never be at rest only by itself; the black body at rest draws other black bodies at rest toward it, draws those other historic bodies into the situation, other bodies that are, on the face of it, totally disconnected from the event at hand—the event that is not discrete because of the ways in which the multiple resonates.[1] The event is only partially—and very rarely—the product of chance. It also marks that not entirely random moment when various historical forces (often antagonistic) come into an unforeseen (unforeseeable), unavoidable conflict. However, the effect of this chance and this history is to provoke multiplicities (what we might also regard, in this instance, as a form of concatenation, linkages across history, likenesses that resonate), many of which are unpredictable, many of which—like the effect of gathering—appear, on the face of it, disconnected. If only for a moment, however, the force of chance renders explicable disconnections unsustainable. What other black bodies at rest does the prostrate African American basketball player Artest call into play, gather to himself? What other multiplicities does he release into play?

As Artest lay supine on the scorer's table, Pistons fans, some of them inebriated, most of them white and male, most of whom were unhappy at Artest's showboating in their building (the Palace at Auburn Hills, on the outskirts of predominantly black Detroit), inserted themselves into the act—sought to make their mark on the incident. Their intensity, of course—the force they brought to bear against Artest and some of his Pacer teammates—is what partially made the event. Physically (throwing beer cups at him, making threatening gestures at him) and verbally (yelling, directing expletives at him), these fans attacked the at-rest Artest both because of his actions (showboating, acting the *voyou*) and for interrupting the action; as a result, the Palace irrupted into the event. A tough player, Artest responded by charging into the stands to find the offending fans; seconds later, he was joined by his teammates Jermaine O'Neal and Stephen Jackson, fellow African Americans intent on protecting their Pacer colleague. A melee ensued as players and fans tussled, and officials found themselves unable to reimpose order on the game.[2]

The effect of Artest's interruption into stasis was ubiquitous. It drew everyone in—from his teammates to opposing players, from NBA officials to hometown fans. Stasis transformed a player-on-player incident into, and initiated, the event: the act of white fans throwing cups of beer onto the spectacularly at-rest black male athlete's body mobilized that body into a violent, transgressive retaliation. The force of subtraction is what we might name its Newtonian magnetism, a force born entirely of the act of an immanent withdrawal into stillness. If every action, as the first law of Newtonian physics states, produces an equal and opposite reaction, then, paradoxically phrased, every black athletic inaction produces an unequal and (hostile) opposite (white) reaction. The usually mobile, athletic black body at rest spurs the usually relatively immobile white body (immobile, except for the expected bouts of cheering or jeering) to action against the body it is not ordinarily able to attack—the body that is obviously, physically, beyond the spectator's capabilities; the body that acts on the basketball court, physically near but far outside the conceptual space of the white spectator; the body that is in time with the basketball clock. It is not that the roles are reversed exactly but that a spectacular black stillness where it is imagined to be out of place—interruption is presumed to be verboten on an NBA court—is intolerable to those who understand black bodies at rest to be a provocation, an act against the order of (athletic and political) things. In Newtonian logic, the act of black interruption can only be met with, gainsaid, acted against, with white irruption.[3] Such is the force of subtraction: this is the only direction in which thinking the event of the black body at rest can go. Just as the "offended" white sedentary spectator in the Palace is drawn, as if inexorably, to the supine (Artest) and in-motion (his teammates) athletic black bodies, so thinking the event (in sport and, possibly, elsewhere) must go toward the subtraction, toward that which seeks to break the bonds of a too-narrow suture so that other connections might be forged, toward that (body) which the multiple releases into possibility, the body that is denied the right to be, if only for a moment, at rest—say, the black self resting in an undesignated area on a bus in Montgomery, Alabama, or the commitment to principled, steadfast immobility that is audible in that civil rights anthem "We Shall Not Be Moved"; or, as famously, John Carlos and Tommy Smith, viscerally disrupting the 1968 Olympic Games in Mexico City with the political force of their Black Power salute. What does the black body have to do to earn the right to be at rest in public (or to raise its fists in a defiant, photogenic, stillness)? Attaining such a right, of course, will always involve political struggle. At the very least, however, we can be sure that (black) subtraction, the act of taking the self out of action, will always be a political challenge—an act of protest or resistance. Black subtraction is never nothing, can never be nothing. There is always something at stake when the black body refuses to mobilize itself publicly—to perform its athleticism, to perform athletically, to play out its political role, especially if that role is to enact its submission or perform its disenfranchisement.

Thinking Artest's body as a suburban Detroit event demands looking critically at that moment in the Palace and that aspect of the violence that occurred at the Palace in a way that does not simply designate it "provocation," all the while recognizing that Artest's *voyou*-ish act of spectacular stillness—"subjugation"—on the scorer's table constitutes an intentional, deliberate provocation of the Pistons fans. In the face of the law's impotence, having rendered the law (momentarily) ineffective, Artest determines: I will not be moved. Artest's deliberate at-restness constitutes a declaration that, naturally, carries within it a (dialectical) coda: I will not be moved without your violence. The black body can only be "restored" to its "proper" actions (movement) through violent reignition—it must defend itself; it must act to defend other black (athletic) bodies under attack. It is for this reason that, as much as the performance of laying supine formed part of that moment, it is not an exhaustive or even sufficient explanation for that crucial interlude—that "intervening episode, period, or space" within the event.[4]

This chapter engages the fracas, which variously became known as the Motown Melee or the Palace Brawl, by recasting it in terms of an event, one capable of recognizing the peculiar problematic of athletic violence as it obtained that night in suburban Detroit—fan against player, player against player, player against fan. To name the event, it is necessary to philosophically immobilize or recast the proceedings of that evening—as the moment/(non)movement of the black body: the black body at rest is the event. It is important to recognize that the event, in this rendering, emanates not from action but instead from spectacular stillness. However, Artest's subtraction from athletic movement, his stillness, does not account fully for, is not the full constitution of, the event. It is necessary, then, both to apprehend the importance of his stillness and to think it, to attach it, to think its concatenation to the event as such.

Thinking the event of Artest as subtraction demands the radical reconception of the time of the event. The event stands not as an intervention—the flagrant foul, the act of spatial transgression (players going into the domain of the spectators)—but as an interruption, which produces a disruption, "concludes" in cessation (momentarily brings everything to a supine, previously unimaginable, unthought-of halt). The event as stasis marks the punctuation of the action, putting an "end" to the action (spectacular stillness)—an end ("I will not be moved") that is, of course, not the end.

In this way, every situation (such as being at rest) within the event contributes to the event in a way that can only be described as potentiality-filled multiplicity. Every situation (S_1) gathers (producing a gathering, G) other situations (S_2) unto itself, leading to an entirely new situation within the event; every situation produces a gathering that produces a new situation; every situation is potentially the event itself. The only way to think about the event, then, is as a simultaneous sequence of S_1–G–S_2. In the event of Artest, the situation of subtraction is the propelling force of the event. It is the situation of subtraction that inaugurates the event; it is when the body stills itself that time, as it were, opens into the event—that the situation gathers time into the event. It is the (force of) subtraction that distinguishes, if this discourse might be permitted, the pre- from the postlapsarian moments in Detroit. It is the spectacular stillness of the black body at rest that separates the final moment of the Pistons–Pacers game (the flagrant foul, S_1) from the violence (G—it gathers all aspects of the NBA game unto itself, from the players and officials to the fans and the stadium's security apparatus to the league's public relations outlet) that ensued; it is subtraction (S_2—the black athletic body at rest) that punctuates, in the sense that it marks an end (if only a putative one) to one modality of action—the game ends, no further action is possible—and inaugurates an entirely new one, S_1–G–S_2, producing the event.

When the athlete subtracts himself from the action, the very movement of the NBA is (temporally) terminated, but, more importantly, it is disrupted into the event; at the very least, a mode of expectation is interrupted. Subtraction precedes Artest's charge into the stands to attack a spectator (John Green, a white fan convicted of a handful of felonies); subtraction precedes his hard foul on Wallace. There can be no subtraction (no "taking away" from that is also an "adding to," that which leads to the making of the event) without punctuation, without the marking, however peremptorily, of a moment's beginning and end. In the Artest instance, the event is unthinkable unless it is understood to proceed from the brief interlude, the situation (S_1), of the black athletic body at rest, what we might think of as the body Artest, the athletic body that arrested itself into the heart of the incident. To invoke a strangely appropriate, neologistic pun, time was "Artested"—arrested, held up, suspended, made discontinuous, by Artest. Time was arrested into, arrested by, arrested as, the event (of) Artest.

The event of the body Artest can only be constituted out of what Badiou offers as a "small temporal truth": that moment when the body Artest refused movement, when it stilled itself spectacularly in public—rendered as part African American spiritual and part Brer Rabbit–like taunting, "I will not be moved / just like a basketball player lying on a scorer's table." A critical part of that "small temporal truth" resides in the singular vulnerability of the black body. The body Artest is not only at rest on the scorer's table but also, unusual for a professional athletic body, exposed without protection to the vituperation of the spectators; the situation (S_1) gathers (G) into the violence that will produce another situation (S_2), "extending," concatenating, or consolidating itself into the event $(S_1–G–S_2)$.

What the event presents us with is the Situation,[5] that constituent of the event (known, less likely, in the moment, or, more likely, in the thinking that follows from and because of the event) that can be properly identified only once it has been, to use a critical term in Heidegger's thinking, "gathered" into the event through its concatenation with another Situation, or an Other or other Situations.[6] The Situation is signal, but it cannot, by itself, constitute the event. The Situation does, however, draw our attention to it—it is something significant that happens, potentially disruptive, potentially irruptive, that might, in its more intense articulation, demand a remark. Because of its relation to the event, the effect of the Situation, even in its less forceful instantiation, is such that it requires a remark.

The Situation is that which, having happened, makes necessary a speaking to it. It then becomes necessary to speak of the Situation. The Situation must then be gathered unto itself, which requires the consideration of both what seems obviously congruent (patently related to it) and, more important, what appears to have no apparent relation to—and no bearing on—the Situation or, it should be said, the event. The Situation is that constituent element of the event that can inflame or instigate the event (set things in motion)—it is never the event. The Situation depends on the Gathering to connect it to another Situation, both the Situation that "belongs" to it and the one that does not "strictly speaking belong to it"; the event does not require a Situation, but the Situation always depends on something other than itself. To become an event, the Situation must be Gathered into, brought together with, something other than itself. The event is always in excess of the Situation; the Situation does not necessarily "aspire" to the event. The event can be, in part, expressed in the formula $E = S_1-G-S_2$ (or a variable number of Situations): the Situation is Gathered into an other—"an other" is not the same as "another" (just one more, just another one) because there is something distinct about the other Situation—Situation or other Situations.[7]

In the aftermath of S_1-G-S_2, the Artest event quickly degenerated into a general condemnation, both implicit and explicit, of the NBA as a "black" league, and this led to a widespread indictment of black male athletes. For this reason, the Artest event demands, following Spinoza, a philosophical reconsideration. The event must be "thought," attended to, made a matter for contemplation, in such a way that it is not "limited by another thought"; thinking the body Artest must not be delimited by the thought that goes by the proper name of denunciation.[8] The event of the body Artest, what the fracas in Detroit has been taken to mean, must not be decided in advance of its having been thought. This "reconsideration" is based on the premise that the "meaning" of the event of stasis is given by the event itself, by thinking the process of S_1–G–S_2—what kind of discursive arrangement and rearrangement takes place each time we turn to the terms of the event?

There can be no reconsideration of the body Artest except to think it as an event, first and foremost, that must be approached through the opacity of refusal, stasis, and subtraction—articulating the event into its own conceptualization. The event of the body Artest must be thought as that critical conflict between action and stillness, that struggle between the athletic body in motion and at rest. What emerges from these struggles, what is gathered into it, is an American conflict that long precedes Artest, a conflict that, in proliferating beyond itself, reveals the unpredictability of the supplement—a supplement, moreover, that can only be thought in and through the effects of subtraction.

Conceived predominantly within a temporal paradigm, the time of being at rest, this chapter recognizes how the logics of temporality and spatiality inform—and often mutually constitute—each other. For this reason, the problematic of how black athletic bodies occupy public space is privileged in order to read how these bodies move in that space and the limitations and possibilities that attach to that mobility. Of equal interest is how Artest's momentary immobility—refusing the demand of perpetual black athletic motion—triggers the release of an enigmatic voice. By being still and speechless (while still, of course, speaking through his body) on the scorer's table, Artest becomes, momentarily, inexplicable. He becomes, in rapid succession, familiar (flagrant foul), then unfamiliar (at rest): an enigma to the officials, his teammates, his opponents, the fans, possibly even himself. (Buried within that sequence might very well be the true force of the event: to make the self unrecognizable to itself.) The tough, skillful, uncompromising, and often mouthy defender (the defender who is always full of fighting talk, or talking "smack," to render it in the vernacular; that is, Artest the *voyou*) Artest was transformed, in that moment, into the voice of rest—the voiceless at rest, but still not silent. At rest but not restful, at rest and still restive, provocative in his restfulness, Artest became the black body that was temporarily supine, not moving, the body that (*voyou*-ish or not) for a momentous second or two refused the perpetual on-court motion that is unthinkingly expected of the NBA athlete.

Finally, in locating Artest in relation to other—historical—black bodies at rest (gathering these bodies together into another situation), a series of questions emerges: is the fact of the black body at rest less problematic than the particular form that that rest takes? Do different forms of immobility, different articulations of "I Shall Not Be Moved," potentially represent a different politics?

Within conventional norms of the flow of what Walter Benjamin names "empty, homogeneous time," the ideologically uninterrupted temporal (and spatial) organization of American sport, certain arrestings of time are permissible: in baseball, the seventh-inning stretch; the traditional moment of rooting for the home team; a moment of silence for those who died in wars or natural disasters before the game; and, of course, time-outs (the suspension of game time; "stopping the clock," as the phrase goes), the unstructured but agential (orchestrated by coaches, although it is sometimes called, or initiated, by players) interruptions—not disruptions—of the homogeneous flow.[9] (Time-outs are unstructured and yet always anticipated, always planned for, as such. Coaches know they will invariably have to call them in response to the flow of the game, normally to interrupt a bad run and give them the opportunity to correct things or to run a special play in a key moment.) Disruptions, however, can transform rest into ideological unrest. These include the body at rest, like Artest's, and those bodies that will make a politically differential, oppositional use of moments of enforced rest such as not standing for the national anthem or saluting the national flag. Here one might cite the now retired Puerto Rican first baseman Carlos Delgado during his tenure with the Toronto Blue Jays. In his time as a Blue Jay (a politics he ameliorated when he later joined the New York Mets from the Florida Marlins), Delgado remained seated in the dugout for the singing of "God Bless America" during the seventh-inning stretch because of his opposition to the bombing target practice performed by the U.S. military on the island of Vieques, Puerto Rico (and his opposition to the Iraq War). Or one might look at instances of refusing and shaming the nation through a salient accoutrement (Carlos and Smith, so unforgettable at the 1968 Olympics, black gloves on their hands for their clenched-fist Black Power salute during the medal ceremony).

These strategies for reencoding rest and converting immobility into the opportunity for symbolic political protest (mobilizing the body at determined rest), these historic bodies at rest, are what the NBA body of Artest is heir to, stands in relation with, is historically gathered into. However, is the disruption of time through symbolically abstracting the body from labor, and flaunting that withdrawal of the body from the NBA's temporal homogeneity, the new millennium's unintended, politically amorphous equivalent of the Black Power defiance of the 1960s? Would such an analogy be accurate? In all probability, the answer would be a resounding no.

The intention here, then, is not to suggest that Artest belongs to the same ideological pantheon as Smith and Carlos, or, for that matter, the heavyweight boxers Jack Johnson and Muhammad Ali (what was all that rhyming and rope-a-dope but the taunting of the *voyou*-ish boxer?), both iconic figures of a critical African American vernacular tradition.[10] It is, rather, to show how resonant the memory of historic black bodies is, how easily black bodies at rest concatenate, how "uneventful" acts of defiance, decades apart, recall other, more obviously political instantiations of black bodies at rest—how these restive bodies come to be, can be, gathered together. Some of those other African American bodies to which the Artestian body draws us have been subtracted from action in arenas—and in historical moments—where the political stakes were infinitely higher, in political conflicts far removed from the privileged confines of an NBA arena. However, the force of subtraction and gathering is such that Artest is at once disconnected from the NBA into a relation not only with his African American athletic predecessors but also with other figures in African American history famous for their acts of stasis—their at-rest protests.

The event of Artest is put into communication with other events, not all of which, as is the nature of gathering, necessarily resemble each other. In this way, the history of the event becomes historical in its relation to—we might even say its dependence on—other events. The event becomes eventful through its supplementarity—its ability to make history by itself and to be illuminated by, to concatenate with, other events, other events it recalls, gathers into itself. Figured historically, the Artest event amounts to, in Deleuze's obviously Heideggerian terms, "a single clamor of Being for all beings."[11] Resonant in the clamor is a call for something other than representation, something more than representation, something that refuses the necessarily circumscribed politics of identity. The Artestian clamor, in its concatenated relation, is infused with the imperative to think what stasis might achieve politically (might we call it "justice," if not for Artest, then for the figures he evokes?); to think justice through the time of the event; to think a justice that begins in subtraction or in the action of subtraction, burnished by the roguish allure of the *voyou*. The call for justice is, in this formulation, most cacophonous in the act of retreat, most visible in spectacular stillness; the law is uncertain about what to do in the face of (*voyou*-ish) stillness. To achieve this notion of justice, it is necessary to understand, following Badiou's rendering of Deleuze, the latter's critical philosophical substitution. Deleuze is "against the sedentary *nomos* of Essences," preferring instead the "nomad *nomos* of precarious actualizations."[12] In place of identity, with its "sedentary *nomos* of Essences," a nomadic order—a *nomos* that is mobile, nimble, adept at rapid movement in (and across) time—must be called into action by subtraction. Caution is required, of course—such is the character of "precarious actualizations." But out of this order there can emerge a fuller account of the event, a more complete but not commensurately equal account of the place of the (sport's) event in history—an account that often works through repetition, a repetition that reveals the inequality at play as well as the precariousness of the concatenation, a more illuminating account of the supplementarity of the sport's event. It is "precarious" to "actualize" the event in this disconnected, historically divergent way, but because of this risk, there is at least the guarantee that subtraction is not submerged beneath the seductive political accoutrements of representation. This is the order, the "sedentary Essence," that must be resisted; this is the *nomos* with which we must be impatient.

THE BODY IN TIME

Like all sports, the NBA is primarily about time. In fact, time—and the art of timing—is so constitutive of "modern" sports, with the fetishization of counting, statistics, and standardization, that sports historians have traced the rise of sport as we technologically know it to the late-nineteenth-century invention of the stopwatch, the most "precise" recording of athletic achievement. It is technology, massively refined in the intervening decades, that now enables statisticians to keep records, which is to say, to keep time, in nanoseconds. It is sport's dependence on time (it is the founding conceptual frame for many sports, from the hundred-meter dash to a five-day international cricket match) that gave rise to those temporally determined phrases that abound in sport. These phrases are so often repeated, mantralike, that they may be said to constitute an ideology. These expressions—such as "managing the clock," "milking the clock," "controlling the clock," and the ultimate unit of temporal measurement, "time of possession"—constitute a staple of sport's lingua franca. All of these phrases encode a simple sport's philosophy: deny the opposition possession of the ball and thus prevent them from scoring. "You can't score without the ball," so the saying goes, invoked with special abandon by coaches, players, and commentators associated with the National Football League (NFL). Central to this thinking is the premise that temporality can be made subservient to the management of sport's authority—officials, coaches, players. So temporally determined is sport that we might argue, given the authority of the clock, that there is a separate temporal dimension: sport's time, the actual time of the game, a configuration of temporality that literally measures every tick of the clock precisely and absolutely, a temporality that conducts itself as not only independent of but also as operating distinct from "real time."

Sport's time, or "game time," has a complicated relationship to real time: while every tick of the clock assumes an exaggerated importance, the actual time of the game conflicts with real time because every interruption, be it an injury (often translated into an official's time-out, the act of metaphorically and literally suspending, if not time, then the time of the game) or a coach's time-out, freezes the movement of the game clock, if not real time. Within sport's temporality, time can be arrested, made to stand still for seconds, minutes—even, in exceptional cases, for hours (in the event of a serious injury, a rain delay, or a natural or structural disaster)[13]—because the sport's clock, the only measure of time that matters, is suspended. Because of the coexistence of these two conceptually discrete temporalities, an NBA game, a scant forty-eight minutes (four twelve-minute quarters), or an hour-long NFL game (four fifteen-minute quarters), or a National Hockey League game (three twenty-minute periods, with a fifteen-minute intermission between each period) can last three or more real hours. Victory or defeat is largely determined by the game clock, a temporality that simulates a real clock, except that it can be "randomly" suspended—thereby extending temporality in ways inimical to real time. In game time, the clock moves too slowly when, especially in a close contest, victory is tantalizingly near and can only be announced when time "runs out," signaling the peculiar finitude of game time—the match is over, according to the clock. Alternately, time moves too fast when defeat stares a team in the face and, the partisans desperately hope, another minute of playing time will surely produce a miraculous victory.

Sport is, in its own formulation, nothing but the experience of living perpetually in a highly particularized, structured, terminal time. (The game will end; the game clock, if not the clock of historical time, will stop ticking.) By refusing perpetual motion in favor of rest, Artest provokes a temporal dilemma. What happens when these two temporalities, already operating in an awkward synchronicity, collide, come into conflict? What does sport's time mean outside its specialized, precisely measured temporality? The NBA is temporally Cartesian: I play, therefore I am. I move, therefore I am. Ergo, when I am still—at rest—what am I? Am I? What kind of inaction is possible outside of movement? To phrase Badiou's assertion as a question, can the "unique voice of Being make itself heard in its multiple declension"?[14] Through the act of lying on the scorer's table, Artest arrested time—he made it stand, almost literally, one might argue, spectacularly still. By acting out of character, voluntarily, playfully, provocatively "submitting" to the authority of the referees who said he had just committed a flagrant foul, Artest was able to control—through his double interruption, first the foul and then languid submission (*voyou*-ish interruption as slowness)—the flow of sport's time. Temporality was, if only for a few moments, subjected to the player's rhythm, wrested from the officials, the coaches, the fans, and even the other players.

To "Artest" time is to make it not only stand still but tick to the rhythm of a different—mostly ignored—clock. The black male body, normally a servant of (NBA or NFL) time, became temporarily its controlling force—the keeper of both game and real time. Subtraction (literally here, by removing, abstracting, the athletic body from the action of the game) not only disrupts but also draws time in/to the body at rest—an especially powerful form of gathering. Through the "Artesting" of time, NBA time was exposed to an extraordinary plenitude. Through his actions, Artest showed that there are many temporalities at play, in play, in any one NBA game. Time, through which the "unique voice of Being" speaks, is multiple in its declension. In the face of withdrawal, official time reveals its susceptibility to multiple declension. It is not the only time that can determine the temporal flow of a game. By resting publicly, by making his stasis a public spectacle, Artest made possible multiple, simultaneous opacities of the black body at rest—that it was arrogant, *voyou*-ishly flaunting itself, or that it was simply recognizing how time could be subverted to its, the black body's, own ends.

In this moment, the enigmatic body Artest comes to speak for other times, other bodies, other histories within a racially bifurcated public space, even beyond NBA arenas where predominantly black bodies perform for predominantly white fans. The body Artest reveals how the black body is conceptually transformed in, and, more pointedly, because of, white public space by the disciplinary logic of sport's time; similarly, the body Artest reframes black physical occupation of white public space by refiguring the temporal machinations of NBA time, by deliberately withdrawing from it, by literally lying down at the very fringe of its authority—just outside, on the margins of, its time, the scorer's table, where just the time of the game is monitored, where the state of the game is tallied, where the officials go to make sure they are keeping proper control of the game. The effect of this subtraction is, at the very least, to slow down the NBA clock; in truth, however, what Artest achieves is closer to suspending that clock, through the inertia that is innate to withdrawal ("making time stand still").

In African American history, especially during the civil rights struggle, deciding to remain inert has always been politically generative—it makes something, the political, happen. This was true when Rosa Parks and Jackie Robinson (as a soldier in the segregated South) refused to give up their bus seats to white passengers and when Mamie Till Bradley decided to allow her son Emmett Till's mutilated, misshapen body to be viewed (by as many as fifty thousand mourners) in Chicago after it was returned from Mississippi. Whether it is Gandhi lying fasting on a bed or Parks's refusal to go to the back of the bus, spectacular stillness provokes a vehement—and, finally, futile—political reaction. Despite the brutality of British imperialism, *Swaraj* was achieved (before there was the disarticulation into India and Pakistan); despite the violent intransigence of racist white southerners, African Americans obtained the franchise in Mississippi, and the Montgomery bus system was integrated; despite the threat of lynching in Mississippi and Bull Connor and his dogs in Alabama, the African American franchise was enshrined, given a new, fuller life by the Civil Rights Act.

Parks's refusal to go to the back of the bus, to give up her rightful seat on a segregated bus in Montgomery, Alabama, produced a 381-day bus boycott, led by Martin Luther King Jr., then minister at Montgomery's Dexter Avenue Baptist Church. Spectacular stillness, remaining inert, produced nothing less than—following hard on the heels of Till's murder in an impoverished county in the Mississippi Delta—the civil rights movement. (The two events are closely linked in the struggle for civil rights: "Till's life ended a little over three months before the inauguration, early in December, of the Montgomery bus boycott—the first major Southern black declaration of war against racial injustice in the era after Reconstruction."[15]) What was supposed to be a one-day bus boycott, intended for the day of Parks's conviction, turned into a protest against Montgomery's City Bus Lines that lasted more than a year.[16] One salient fact about Parks's principled inertia is, as she recalls in her autobiography, that she was not sitting out of place. As Taylor Branch explains in *Parting the Waters,* his account of the civil rights movement,

All thirty-six seats of the bus [Rosa Parks] boarded were soon
filled, with twenty-two Negroes seated from the rear and
fourteen whites from the front. Driver J. P. Blake, seeing a
white man standing in the front of the bus, called out for the
four passengers on the row just behind the whites to stand
up and move to the back. Nothing happened. Blake finally
had to get out of the driver's seat to speak more firmly to the
four Negroes. "You better make it light on yourselves and let
me have those seats," he said. At this, three of the Negroes
moved to stand in the back of the bus, but Parks responded
that she was not in the white section and didn't think she
ought to move. She was in no-man's-land. Blake said the white
section was where he said it was, and he was telling Parks
that she was in it.[17]

Rosa Parks was challenging the arbitrariness, and the Blakean
(arbitrary white) sovereignty, if you will, of Alabama law. By
announcing that she would remain in her seat, she was doing
nothing but insisting on her right to keep her place, a place the
law assigned her: "Parks responded that she was not in the white
section and didn't think she ought to move." It was racist southern
custom that Parks stood against, a position Blake recognized: "As
he saw the law, the whole idea of no-man's-land was to give the
driver some discretion to keep the races out of each other's way.
He was doing just that."[18] It was Blake's imagined, historically
unchallenged (or rarely protested) right to discretionary powers
that was intolerable to Parks. She was within her rights; he was
abrogating them simply because he wanted "to keep the races
out of each other's way." He was doing what he thought custom
entitled him to; she, alone of the four affected passengers, refused
southern custom because it constituted an attack on her right to
sit where the law permitted.

Recalling the event of the evening of December, 1, 1955, in
Rosa Parks: My Story, she casts her refusal with greater militancy:

> I was sitting in the front seat of the colored section of a bus in Montgomery, Alabama. . . . More white people got on, and they filled up all the seats in the white section. When that happened, we black people were supposed to give up our seats to the whites. But I didn't move. The white driver said, "Let me have those front seats." I didn't get up. I was tired of giving in to white people.[19]

She was more "tired" than her fellow Negro passengers; more committed to, in this instance, not moving. On December, 1, 1955, Parks was determined that she would not submit to custom—she would remain in her lawful place when, as a rule, "black people were supposed to give up [their] seats to the whites."

Jackie Robinson, too, was "tired of giving in to white people." For all the public admiration for his restraint in the face of racism in Major League Baseball (MLB) from opponents and teammates, Robinson had long since established a reputation as a man with a fiery disposition. He may have (more or less) kept it under wraps during his MLB playing days, but in 1946, Robinson, before he broke the color line in baseball, committed a similar act to Parks's when he refused to give up his seat on a military bus to a white soldier.

In this way, spectacular stillness constitutes, across the decades, a uniquely African American event in which, according to Deleuze in a way that builds on Heidegger's notions of gathering and *Enteignis* (dispersion), "all events communicate with each other" and, in the process, "attain the radicalness of the disjunctive synthesis."[20] There is nothing that concatenates these events—a bus boycott, a military refusal (two militant refusals), and a supine basketball player—except the force of their historical communication, except the disjunctive way in which they compel a historicized synthesis. Disjunctive synthesis marks a coming together, a congregating, for a moment, together in the radical, perpetual present that is the event of spectacular stillness.[21] These events (Robinson, Parks, Till, and Artest) "attain" each other, subtract—remove themselves, withdraw—from the present into each other, into their eventfulness—the radical synthesis that is not at first apparent but is revealed in thinking the event of black bodies being at rest. Rosa Parks and Ron Artest (and Jackie Robinson, we might add) do not, in any usual sense, belong together, except that they share in—are gathered into, are disjunctively joined by—the event of radical subtraction. In this conceptualization, the black body (or bodies) that will not vacate its (or their) seat joins the black body in stasis: "We Shall Not Be Moved." S_1–G–S_2 (or multiple S_2s): out of the situations in this multiple process emerges, it is possible to argue, the opacity of stasis as event in contemporary African American history: to be at rest shows itself to be the event, across events, disjunctively synthesizing situations. The event of stasis as such performs two functions: it shows how the civil rights struggle as event, as variously incarnated in Parks and Robinson, makes possible—may even demand—the subtraction of Artest from "mere" suture to sports and reconnects it to the multiple other registers in which the event resonates, and it reveals those other registers in all their unexpectedness. The event of stasis makes philosophical movement (from situation to situation, from event to event) possible, perhaps even imperative. The event must never be sutured to its own discourse; that is what makes the event unthinkable; it is the event of at-rest-ness that compels thinking toward the event of stasis. The event is always (prone to) rearranging things, primarily our thinking of it. The event offers us resources, not least among them political, historical, and philosophical, for remembering or deploying originary truisms. That is, the event is what gives us to thinking; or it is the movement against originary stasis that inclines toward the at-rest-ness that brings us to thought.

All this notwithstanding, in the political iconography of African Americans, Parks and Artest could hardly be farther apart. Parks was not the first Negro to be arrested for refusing to obey a bus driver's command, but she was, without question, by far the most exemplary community member to be "booked, fingerprinted, and incarcerated"[22] for doing so. In Reverend King's estimation, Parks was "one of the finest citizens in Montgomery—not one of the finest Negro citizens—but one of the finest citizens in Montgomery." Only because of her unimpeachable standing in black Montgomery—a stature that King extends to Montgomery in its entirety—was it possible to make her conviction the test case for challenging the law. Parks's exemplarity allowed King and the civil rights campaigners to make the law stand stronger, more powerful, than southern custom (to make the law undo itself, to remake itself as a law that could sustain itself; to make a law as Law beyond arbitrary white sovereignty—Law that had to be recognized by all, that gave all the right to sit wherever they chose).

Under no circumstances can Artest be thought in such an elevated fashion. However, the failure to recognize how staying in one's seat (Parks, Robinson) is bonded to retreat (Artest and Parks are connected here through disjunctive synthesis) derives solely from the refusal—or the inability—to think the event as its own particular form of political communication—to recognize how, in its dispersion, the event gathers that which does not appear to properly, if at all, belong to it: those historical moments, the event into the event (if we can, for a moment, conceive of the Civil Rights Act symptomatically, as the event of justice).

In this thinking of the event, it is of little, if any, consequence that one figure is an exemplary member of the community, beyond reproach, an icon in the struggle for civil rights, and that the other stands well outside that political orbit. It matters only that the event—the historic event of stasis, more importantly—excludes nothing, evokes everything. It is out of this event that the event of spectacular stillness can produce an unlikely African American triumvirate of spectacular stillness (Till's inertia is excluded, located later in a different relation to Artest) that begins with a soldier canonized in American history for his tolerance for ignoring racism both on and off the baseball diamond, reaches its apogee with a Montgomery seamstress, and takes on its most unexpected declension with an NBA player—three Situations Gathered by, and into, the event. (As the vagaries of history would have it, Artest chooses inertia in suburban Auburn Hills, just a few miles from the Detroit housing project where Rosa Parks lived from 1957 onwards, and where she died.) These are the faces of a radical congregation, gathered in their unexpected disjunctiveness—a disjunctiveness that is marked, as Derrida correctly insists, by a "mutual belonging" that bears within it an historic tension.

These bodies in subtraction are not simply concatenated; in tension they may be, but they are all members of an eternal congregation. They are not merely linked by the event (of no small significance in itself, to be sure). They constitute a congregation: theirs are bodies bound together in the most predictable or unlikely ways, for all eternity; they are always in communion with one another, a communing of the black political. In Parks's case, there is also a very specific commitment to a Christian ethic. The force of the eternal, the logic of a form of religiosity, if you will, allows for the overcoming of the disjunctive synthesis; the disjunctive synthesis is resolved by—and in—eternity. At the very least, the canonization of Parks and Robinson reveals the eternal nature of their standing in American and African American life. (In this regard we may say that the fourteen-year-old Till marks a special case. Because he was a victim of white vigilante violence, augmented by the refusal of the all-white Sumner County jury to convict the perpetrators, the half brothers Roy Bryant and J. W. Milam, he was made a martyr by history. The actions that led to his murder, be it the "wolf whistle" at the white woman, Carolyn Bryant, or the supposed advances he made to her, remain forever shrouded in mystery. They are the acts of an urban— Chicago—teenager regarded as intolerable in the rural enclaves of the Deep South.)

The act of stillness, the event of (African American) subtraction, acting (or political movement) through subtraction, provokes what Deleuze names "perpetual reconcatenation." This is a mode of Deleuzian communication—there can be no thinking that is not also, fundamentally, a communication—that does more than perpetually bind Artest to the history of spectacular African American stillness, to Robinson, Parks, and Emmett Till. The communication among these and other figures suggests not only that they will be perpetually concatenated but also that their concatenation is perpetually subject—or open—to reconcatenation. Every act of spectacular stillness reorganizes, revivifies (every act makes every other previous act come alive again), every act that came before; moreover, reconcatenation invites another thinking, a new concatenation, of how every act of spectacular stillness stands in relation to—communicates with—every other such act. This is an instance of Deleuzian "double movement,"[23] back and forth, between acts, among acts, of subtraction. (Back and forth between concatenation and congregation: a conceptually thin line divides the two.) The body at rest is never, philosophically, at rest; this body is always on the cusp of not only movement but double movement—movement toward subtraction, concatenated with other, more politically vaunted acts of subtraction; no subtraction can be immunized against a gathering into other subtractions. Appropriate, then, that Badiou deems Deleuze's perpetual reconcatenation the consequence of an "athletic trajectory of thought."[24] In the case of this subtraction, it is the athlete whose trajectory is the most unlikely and, for that reason, the most philosophically arduous.

This is also, however, a double movement that cannot know precisely, if at all, what form the next movement will take, where the next move will be made, or, for that matter, who will make the next move or how that movement will reconcatenate to a movement now lost in the past, the movement whose time has not yet come, even when the event has already passed. Through the movement that has not yet been made, the event can return, can be returned. Here Badiou's work on fidelity is especially apropos. In *Ethics* he argues for the "consistency of a fidelity to a fidelity,"[25] a line of thinking given new vivacity and strength in the *Clamor of Being*: "Fidelity to the event is the militant recollection— transiently obscure and reduced to its actuality."[26] Recollection of, which is also a reconnection to, the event is itself an act of militancy; recollection is never simple, never simply a recollection, marking a return to. Through militancy, transience is overcome. For Parks—a seamstress, on a bus, determined to remain in her seat—militancy arose directly out of physical and political exhaustion: "I was tired of giving in to white people." Once exhaustion sets in, transience and obeisance are put aside. Southern racism has no effective political response to black at-rest-ness.

Etymologically speaking, the black body is no longer obeisant. Rosa Parks will not comply with the arbitrariness of Blake's law. No longer will the black body be deferent to, give itself up to, the voice of a liminal white authority that can induce a profound sense of precariousness and, of course, injustice in the black passenger's sensibility; spectacular stillness challenges, publicly and therefore fatally, the law that gives the white bus driver the right to speak as its arbitrator (which is to say, the law, in this instance, is revealed in its full arbitrariness), the law with the customary power to make the black body move even when it is in its (own) place. Once obeisance is refused, the event is assigned its name— "Rosa Parks," "Ron Artest"—and can take its proper place in history. Through the militancy of spectacular stillness, the actuality of the event is recovered. Inherent in reconcatenation, as in congregation, is an indisputable, recoverable militancy. Militancy can be recollected, made into a fashion entirely unthought— unthinkable to—in its original formulation. In recollection resides the irrepressible possibility of reconcatenation: making militancy; giving militancy names it would not, at first, if ever, identify as its own, names always potentially inimitable to the original collection. Unbeknownst to Rosa Parks, she was establishing, a priori, before it knew itself as such, the Artestian principle as first law of the civil rights movement. Parks was not insisting on her right to the franchise, or to equal protection before the law, that is, the end of Jim Crow, but she claimed for herself—and all other blacks (in their role as commuters, at the very least)—the right of the black body to be at rest. The black body, like all other

American bodies, had the right to stay in its place. Rosa Parks made the right to spectacular stillness sacrosanct. In the Artestian principle resides the incandescence, phrased (or contracted) here to an iconic singularity, of that famous civil rights promise: "I will not be moved"—to which we must add, "Just like Rosa Parks sitting in her seat in a Montgomery, Alabama, bus." Unbeknownst to Artest, by withdrawing to a scorer's table in an NBA game decades later, he gathered himself into the first law of the civil rights movement. In the act of (*voyou*-ish) retreat, Artest joined a hallowed congregation: the church of Rosa Parks, an institution formed in the shadow of Emmett Till's stilled, dead body.

The subtraction that is spectacular stillness takes on a whole number of inflected forms; in its declension, it assumes—is given, takes on—an array of names. In rough chronological order, these names might be said to include Robinson, Parks, the Montgomery bus boycott, the civil rights movement, Carlos, Smith, and Artest. These are all names that, in their being thought together, in their being brought together (gathered in recovery), articulate as the "ontology of the multiple." These names constitute the ontology of the unexpected, names that in their speaking insist that spectacular stillness can never be subsumed, can never be known without declension, can never be denied militancy. Every particular form of stillness gives its name to the event so that stillness can never achieve singularity (it can never be the One; it is always, unfailingly, the multiple, the event). Instead, every event inflects stillness with a particularity that is simultaneously indebted to the force of repetition and entirely marked by its own concatenated spectacularity; spectacular stillness invariably makes imperative a return to the first act: subtraction. If, as Heidegger argues, "all the work of the hand is rooted in thinking" (where we might understand the "hand" to function as a synecdoche for the writing, that is, thinking, B/being), then it could be said that the act of subtraction (as opposed to, in this instance, Heidegger's more passive notion of withdrawal, whose primary function is to shelter), in which is all the work of the body at rest, is rooted in thinking.[27] In the work of the hand, it is possible to see the thinking of justice, the thinking against injustice, coming visibly into its own.

For Rosa Parks and Jackie Robinson, in particular, the following could be claimed: all the work of the unmoving black bottom is the root of civil rights thinking, or the black bottom at rest roots civil rights thinking. As Martin Luther King Jr. so deliberately phrased it in his inaugural address as president of the Montgomery Improvement Association (the organizing committee of the bus boycott), "as we proceed with our program—let us think on these things."[28] When the black bottom will not move, it compels the black political—in this case, the incipient civil rights movement, the program to come—to make thinking immanent. There can be no program for civil rights that is not grounded—before all else, King knows—in thinking. In the civil rights struggle, however, thinking emerges not in the lofty Heideggerian hand but, at the risk of inviting ridicule, in the black bottom. Moreover, in the black bottom—so often a source of scatological humor in black life—there resides, at once, a thinking and a "latent eternity."[29] Rosa Parks's spectacular stillness restores dignity—and thought, or restores dignity through thought—to the black bottom, because that is where all things civil rights begin.

Out of thinking subtraction can spring forth, yet again, the eternal life of the event. What is the event but a form of thinking eternal political life? In the event, everything, alive and dead, can come back to life. When the black body sits or lies down—the things about which King urges a thinking—a politics arises. From the black bottom on the seat, the black bottom that will not give up its seat (when this is the followed custom; when other black bottoms, three to be precise, move to accommodate arbitrary white dictates), there arises a black political that is nothing but subtraction; at the very least, it is subtraction first and foremost. Remaining on the seat, staying in the place assigned, staying within the confines of the law (the law that knows itself only as absolute sovereignty; the law almost unwilling to know its southern self for fear of contradiction and self-indictment), initiates the subtraction of the black bottom into the black political that will gather—disjunctively synthesize—the entire American nation up into civil rights.

TWO ASPECTS

For the black athletic body to be at rest is to disrupt the expectations of perpetual performativity in the NBA. To be at rest is to subtract (unsuture) Artest from himself, to make him a part—or Other—to himself, of himself in the duration. Subtraction, in this instance, is the process by which the relentless, insistently mobile defender, the perfectly positioned, athletic rebounder, is momentarily transformed into the figure of (performed) quiescence. Not, it should be stressed, acquiescence, but quiescence, the act of withdrawing the black body from motion into stillness and inactivity—the black body, motionless. And there is nothing *voyou*-ish about absolute stillness as it obtains here, however much the decision to enact rest was *voyou*-ishly conceived. In terms of Deleuze's work on the cinema, "movement has two aspects. On the one hand, that which happens between objects or parts; on the other hand that which expresses the duration or the whole. The result is that duration, by changing qualitatively, is divided up in objects, and objects, by gaining depth, by losing their contours, are united in duration."[30] Artest can be understood as the object or part that changes qualitatively in the course of, and in its relationship because of, the duration—the time of the cinematic whole.[31]

To be at rest is to initiate a politics not through confrontation, such as hard-nosed defending or even the flagrant foul, but through stillness. By subtracting its mobile part from itself (taking itself out of the action, out of the equation of perpetual movement) and remaining inert, the black body becomes the act of a spectacular stillness. In spectacular stillness, the body makes itself, in a Deleuzian fashion, cinematic. In its apprehension, the

body demands that it be looked at; that its stillness, its motion-
lessness, be contemplated; that it be thought, thought on terms
disconnected from its former (recognizable) articulation. At rest,
the black body disembodies—disarticulates—itself from its prior
self. At rest, the athletic body becomes a plenitudinous—making
possible the multiple—disruption of the athletic spectacle that
is the NBA; the athletic body at rest is a spectacular generator of
thought. When players, officials, and spectators in the NBA are
faced with deliberate (political) inaction (inactivity) where relentless activity is expected, they are at a loss what to do. As all the
participants know, opposing players cannot stay in the lane for
more than three seconds; no more than two players on defense
can be in the paint—the area beneath the basket—unless they
are guarding an opponent. "Move, move, move" could easily be
the mantra of the NBA. ("Move," as in "remove yourself to the
place I—Blake—deem proper for you in this instance," is precisely
the injunction that Rosa Parks would not follow.)

By occupying the scorer's table, Artest freezes time in precisely
the place where it is kept and interrupts the tabulation of the game
itself. The scorer's table is the physical site—and site of citation—
that is inside, a part of, and outside the game. By occupying the
table in studied, even self-pleasuring repose, Artest (with)draws
the entire framework and functioning of the game into question.
This throws into sharp relief relations between—the mutual dependence of—the object and the duration. The object, the black
athletic body, terminates the duration of the game. Without the
object, there can be no game.

By withdrawing onto the scorer's table, the body Artest demonstrates how "movement relates the objects of a closed system to
open duration, and duration to the objects of the system which it
forces to open up."[32] Withdrawal, movement (toward) that culminates in stillness, forces the system (NBA) to open itself up; once
time has, momentarily, been called on the system, once game time
has been disconnected/unsutured from itself and opened into a
plenitude of temporalities (culminating in what we might think

of as the time of subtraction confronting the time of the fan), the relationship of object to duration, the two objects of movement (opposing players), must be rethought. As Deleuze argues, "through movement the whole is divided up into objects, and objects are re-united in the whole, and indeed between the two 'the whole' changes."[33] Spectacular stillness, unlike minor challenges (in the NBA the Situation or the incident is not the event), is the radical qualitative change that the duration cannot endure because it compels the termination of game time; spectacular stillness threatens to change the whole to such an extent that the system will be unrecognizable to itself.[34]

The court of ordered athletic NBA movement becomes, because of the event, the melee in Motown. The effect of the event, as Badiou famously argues, is that it "brings to pass 'something other' than the situation, opinions, instituted knowledges; the event is a hazardous [*hasradeux*], unpredictable supplement, which vanishes as soon as it appears."[35] The event produces a hazardous termination, forcing the game to pass into a "something other than usual" end to an NBA game. (In disrupting the game, Artest hazarded his own future, put his livelihood at risk.) The force of the event is both that it makes the event of stillness vanish and that it makes impossible any outcome other than the melee; in this way, the supplement is both unpredictable, impossible to know what will happen because of spectacular stillness, and predictable, because once the NBA's temporality has been superseded by the event, something hazardous is by far the more likely outcome. It is only by keeping faithful (what Badiou names *fidelity,* a "sustained investigation of the situation"[36]) to the event that it becomes possible to know—to produce a "situated knowledge" of the event—that when there is an end to the game that is not an identifiable end to the game, there is no end to the number, the multiplicities, of temporalities that can come into being. The Situation that ensues can know itself only in its unpredictability, which may be the first articulation of fidelity. Because of the event that vanished into a hazardous supplementarity, everyone is, as it were, off the clock, released from the system (the whole has been wholly opened up), free to do with his time as he sees fit.[37] Every actor is released into an act of supplementarity that is unthinkable without the event. What distinguishes the event is its supplementarity. It is supplementarity that makes the event what the Situation can never be: the producer of a hazardous unpredictability, threatening the whole, subtracting the event into the event of civil rights. Here stasis produces political addition.

The Situation can be accommodated by the duration, and the event, by virtue of being an event, overwhelms the duration. The event not only marks the opening up of the system but also announces—makes dramatically visible—the system's limits. The moment at which the system opens up is opened up by the movement toward subtraction (there can be no subtraction that is not preceded, produced by, movement), is opened up by the object's refusal to move, is the juncture at which the system reflexively seeks to close off the opening. It is at this moment that the system not only seeks to reimpose itself as the whole but also seeks its (re)validation; this is the moment at which the system turns, as swiftly as possible, to the law.

Movement can (only) change the relations between objects. The effect of stillness is infinitely greater. It simultaneously changes relations between objects and disables the system. The system cannot function in the face of a spectacular subtraction; subtraction (like the labor strikes that marked the industrial relations between capital and labor) is a time that is sovereign only to itself, no longer subject to the system; subtraction marks the terminal point in the system's duration.

In this way, the body at rest can exceed expectations of itself (as much as it exceeds the system) by allowing critics to conceive, as Kierkegaard might have it, of those issues that are greater than the Artestian body, the body at rest. The body under control, the body in repose, the body that can accept legitimate punishment—for the flagrant foul—is the body that subtracts (unsutures), if only momentarily, the historic Artest (the much-suspended player) from himself (the player who understands the rules even as he contravenes them). For two entangled reasons, the black body at rest is, for white spectatorship, the intolerable black body: first, the body in subtraction (the body made unrecognizable by subtraction; the body unsutured from its own previous discursive apparatus), the body at rest, is systemically intolerable. Artest, 2003–4 NBA Defensive Player of the Year who defended absolutely (from the first second of the game until, literally, the last) against the Pistons in suburban Detroit is now prone to being attacked, without consideration for his vulnerability, by white fans, many of whom were inebriated, especially the culprit-in-chief, John Green; or Artest was attacked, on the receiving end of the half-filled plastic beer cup Green threw at him, precisely because he is vulnerable. This is the body that has reconfigured the whole by drawing the fans toward him (an inexorable invitation, apparently; an invitation to make public the athlete's susceptibility to fan violence), through his subtraction, into the time and space of an NBA game. The whole that emerges from the subtracted body is not coterminous with the NBA's (black) whole. Second, the black body at rest registers as the provocative body, the body whose flaunting of its restfulness is read, sometimes accurately, as taunting, directed at the opposing fans—and, in Artest's case, at supporters of the defeated team.[38]

In the cultural economy of the NBA (and all other sports the world over), it is presumed to be the right of the fans to taunt, provoke, insult, and abuse players; it's all included in the (not inconsiderable) price of admission. Within the racial economy of the NBA, however, it is ironic that, in attacking Artest, the white Detroit fans are symbolically exacting revenge for the loss suffered by "their" black team by attacking a black player on the opposing team. In this event, race, partisanship, and class animus all simultaneously complicate and animate each other, revealing fandom as nothing but a complex of (sustainable, apparently) ideological contradictions. In the event, the political of fandom is patently evident.

The figure of the body at rest constitutes the most salient aspect of the Situation. If, in Badiou's argument about the event, the event is only understood in terms of supplementarity, then the Situation (which remains as such, a constituting nonevent, if you will, until it is gathered into the event) is less improperly understood than singularly unrecognized. The Situation avoids scrutiny—or is ignored—because it is imagined to precede the event and is therefore a priori (and, perhaps because of this, inconsequential) to the event. In the Artest event, however, the Situation is the event. The spectacularly still body is the event. The spectacularly still body reveals that it is Artest's subtractive practice, not his flagrant foul, his infelicitous if not illegitimate (within the context of the game) act, that spurs violence, his own violence and that of others—of fans at the Palace and of other Pacers and Pistons players. The subtraction after the foul can only, then, be conceived as the event; the event must not be surpassed into history, into memory, into the status of the Situation (now anything but a nonevent) by the raucous and violent "something other" of supplementarity.

It was Artest's move toward rest, which, provocative or not, at no point involved physical aggression toward anyone, fan or opposing player, that disrupted that precarious pact of nonphysical confrontation between player and fan. It was precisely the irreconcilability of Artest's two different acts that spawned the event. How could the player, so capable of roughhousing on the court, withdraw, so quickly after the foul, into spectacular stillness? The question, then, is twofold. First, what is the political force of subtraction? And, second, how is it possible that subtraction can overwhelm everything that follows, or goes before?

The Fall into violence, initiated by the Detroit fan(s), is preceded by the act of being at rest. The moment of rest represents the prelapsarian moment, the moment before the Fall that is also, literally, the moment before the Ascent into violence: Artest's ascent into the stands to attack the fans who had attacked him. On the other side of the Ascent, of course, is the professional Fall into the violence that would produce his banishment, for a record seventy-three games, costing him five million dollars in salary. The black body at rest is conceptually inassimilable within the discourse of the NBA because of the offense it gives (fans) and, less frequently reflected on, the vulnerability (of the black bodies that) it engenders—that follows from the Ascent. For Artest, the Fall into infamy signals the movement from the F/fall into the event, the movement from the Situation into the excessive supplementarity that only an event can produce.

The body at rest, the act of lying supine (face up, inert, inactive but by no means passive) on the scorer's table, is a unique event in the NBA. As the Motown Melee showed, however, the black body at rest is a vulnerable entity. Erect, in motion, the body can protect itself. In motion on the court, the body is protected, within the confines of the rules of the game (the rules that could be overridden by custom—in Parks's case, by the arbitrary decision of J. P. Blake, who deemed himself an extension of the law, one who could make the law as it seemed appropriate to him—or, more directly, with the power to act as the law, in the form of a white southern bus driver), by referees and the imagined sanctity of the court. The court is the players' realm, the space where their physical superiority is publicly on display, a spectacle for consumption, desire, and vituperation. The court is not only the space of the spectacle; it is the space prohibited to, out of bounds for, the fans. Within the discursive paradigm that is the NBA, space is racially organized, divided between the "black court" and the "white arena."

If trauma, in Cathy Caruth's terms, is "spoken in a language that is somehow always literary," then basketball, like all American sport, is always spoken in a language that is historically racialized.[39] Race and racism are already sutured to the language of sport, not only in the United States but everywhere. Sport is the language, moreover, that both the players and the fans understand, a tacit agreement in which both are complicit and complicitously aware of the history that has produced not only the NBA and MLB but also the discordance between the material conditions—the housing projects of Cabrini-Green (now demolished) in Chicago and Queensbridge in New York City—where the likes of Artest learn their skills and hone their trade, and the plush environs, such as Madison Square Garden in New York (where Artest played his home college games for St. John's University) or the Staples Center in Los Angeles (where Artest starred for the Los Angeles Lakers;[40] where he won an NBA Championship in 2010), where these African American players ply their trade.

"The possibility of knowing history," writes Caruth, "is thus also raised as a deeply ethical dilemma: the unremitting problem of *how not to betray the past*."[41] For African American athletes, especially those from the pathologized inner city, Caruth's traumatic past—and the dilemma of betrayal that inheres in it—articulates itself as the conflict between, on one hand, the space of origin and, on the other, the class ascension that the materially privileged life of an NBA player represents. This ethical dilemma is most frequently cast as the influence of hip-hop within the game—the struggle that NBA players who are would-be rap artists, such as Artest, have to keep current their racial and cultural authenticity, the struggle to remain true to their childhood neighborhood ('hood), the struggle to maintain credibility in the likes of Cabrini-Green or Queensbridge or inner-city Baltimore. This conflict between past and present, poverty and wealth, urban violence and suburban safety (a myth rudely shattered by the Palace Brawl because it rendered porous the boundaries between economically devastated, postindustrial Detroit and the well-heeled suburbs that surround the erstwhile Motor City), is another way in which the many iterations of mobility—as metaphor for class ascension, as antithesis of being at rest—return to haunt the black athletic body and psyche. Mobility finds articulation as the conundrum that will allow the black athletic body, almost literally, no resting place, the process that expects the inner-city body to be perpetually in motion between the court and the ghetto, the suburbs and the ghetto, to always think the linkage between Queensbridge and

Madison Square Garden. In the popular rendering of the inner city, the price for betrayal is to be culturally outlawed, denigrated by the 'hood for leaving the 'hood, named Other—or worse, in inner-city argot. Players such as Carmelo Anthony (born in New York City, where he now plays for the Knicks), famous for his loyalty to his inner-city Baltimore roots (Anthony moved there when he was seven), have been taken to task for their continued relationship to the originary community, for tending their relationship to the street—for not, as it were, abandoning the street to its proper place (the past), for continuing to remain in motion between one site and another.

The black athletic body that is Artest's (or Anthony's) is expected to negotiate not only its (relationship to) time—its on-court timing, when to make cuts, the exact millisecond that it can take a charge and earn the team a turnover, another valuable possession, when to concede a cheap or flagrant foul—but the ethical relationship between time and space. Within the history that is the black body, the logics of temporality and spatiality coincide, overlap, and complicate each other. For the black athletic body, especially the materially privileged but psychically still-rooted-in-the-place-of-origin body, there are few, if any, moments of rest, moments in which they can be at rest. Like the ubiquity of the always-ticking clock, ticking on the play, on the game, on the series, on the season, where there is no outside, so, too, there is no outside of the condition of the black body. There is, reductively phrased, no outside of blackness, certainly not in the NBA, whatever (postracial) fictions the Michael Jordan NBA spawned.

THE TIME OF THE NBA LAW

At rest on the scorer's table, the body can be ruthlessly attacked. Worse, the black athletic body is not, by the law of the NBA, permitted to defend itself. Black bodies can be the target of onslaught, with no right to respond—certainly not in kind. There resides, in the moment at rest, the latent power of physicality that is ambivalent in its functioning. Contained within the moment of restfulness is also the potential for restiveness—for the unleashing of violence by both, or either, spectators and players. Artest's moment of rest catalyzed this propensity for latent racialized resentments—the white suburban fans angered by the swagger of black players, a pose sine qua non in everyday American life; the anger of the black player attacked for being black—that articulated itself as an eventful violence. The body Artest ignited the event: a minority of identifiable black bodies, the players—punishable by virtue of their recognizability—engaging a multitude of anonymous white bodies. As journalist Terry Maxwell, cryptically but tellingly, inquires, "If race wasn't an issue, why didn't the black fans join with the white fans to vent their hostility toward the Pacer players?"[42] The suburban Detroit brawl was, among an array of reasons, an unsightly spectacle. It staged an unequal drama, pitting the honed athlete against the out-of-shape suburbanite, each bristling with his own antagonisms, resentments normally cloaked by the civility of sport as consumer spectacle.

Into the supplementarity of the event stepped, with no sense of historical self-reflexivity, the NBA commissioner, David Stern, a minuscule, unathletic white man ruling—often like a czar—his predominantly black charges. Pronouncing his decision like a Roman emperor of old or with the vainglorious sensibility of a Third World dictator, Stern the Sovereign's verdict was, literally, the Word made law: "It was unanimous, one to nothing. I did not strike from my mind the fact that Ron Artest had been suspended on previous occasions for loss of self-control."[43] Acting imperiously (much more so than J. P. Blake, who had to call in the police to enact the law), Stern punished Artest not only for his transgression at the Palace but also, evoking the 1990s California law that had such a baseball ring to it ("three strikes and you're out," applied liberally to predominantly minority bodies, whatever the nature of their offense), for those crimes for which the then-Pacer player had already paid his dues—literally in cash and in the games for which he was suspended. Stern's NBA word is not only law, it is also the concatenated history of the law. Artest's history in the NBA, his previous infractions, was reactivated into the life of the event (so that every incident in the NBA is always susceptible to having a Stern—a commissioned—afterlife), was written into the severity of the Stern legal decree. The NBA commissioner alone, as the unimpeachable sovereign, appends value to crimes, his designation of transgressions determinate—the sole, unaccountable (except to the owners and the fans) voice of white authority. His decisions alone have the force of law.

In basketball terms, for the 2004–5 season, Artest was not only five million dollars lighter in the wallet, he had also gone rapidly from being the body at rest to being the metaphorically (and professionally) dead black athletic body, invoking the memory of other publicly dead black bodies. The body at rest, which had made the body vulnerable, was now the Pacer player non grata—the player without standing in the NBA. As Artest was a publicly dead black body, his moment of lying supine contained within it a prescience—the not-yet-dead body anticipating its own public demise—about his professional fate. However, in that moment of being at rest, Artest demonstrated how black bodies can exceed their own metaphysical death in contradictory ways. What are we to make of black bodies who, in public, offer themselves up for death?

On one hand, in the process of being attacked, the vulnerable body makes itself punitively exemplary. The punished body, à la Artest or Sprewell (Latrell Sprewell, who, as a player for the Golden State Warriors, once choked his coach, for which he received a hefty suspension), is the instructive body, the body whose transgressions are used to signal the danger of falling foul of the law. The punished body speaks to, but also for, other potentially transgressive bodies. In Stern-speak, "the line is drawn and my guess is that it won't happen again—certainly not by anybody who wants to be associated with our league."[44] The law is, as it must be to stand, declarative: "The line is drawn and my guess is that this won't happen again." The force of the Word of the law is that it, being the law, can undercut itself by casting itself, in short order, as declarative, that is, sovereign, and then as a punitive speculation—"my guess is." Only the law can wager against its own sovereignty. Only the law can use the speculative "my guess" as a harbinger of its own unchallengeable authority.

However, the law may have reason to indulge in speculation. Publicly disciplined, the black athletic body exceeds itself. The punishment enacted against the black body is always metonymic. The law can only function in part, against a part; it cannot act against the All. It is for this reason that the law is designed to be exemplary in both the hardship imposed and the labor spared by (the NBA commissioner as singular authority) making the "deviant" one (be it Artest or Sprewell) stand in for the many (the vanilla conformists, such as Tim Duncan [San Antonio Spurs] or Grant Hill [Los Angeles Clippers; now retired], both of them law-abiding citizens of the NBA, and the potential transgressors). Conversely, the black body that is publicly punished, either figuratively or metaphorically mutilated, recalls other historic black bodies that have suffered similar fates. In the acerbic, historically resonant terms of one critic, "we have now witnessed the public hanging of Ron Artest, with Stern playing the role of sheriff."[45] In this indictment of Stern, there are powerful echoes of other black bodies that have been mutilated, disfigured, and publicly flogged in American history—injustice meted out, no less, by the ultimate figure of wanton, renegade justice in the American popular imaginary: the sheriff of the frontier West(ern) who appropriates to himself the right not only to impose but to make the Law.

If Artest is already a congregant with Parks and the civil rights movement, then the invocation of a public hanging cannot but release into hermeneutic play the ghosts of other historic, other acted-against, black bodies and racist practices; still, of course, such an enunciation must include a word of caution about attending to the discreteness of the historical moments. (Though Situations can be gathered together, they are not by any means historically equal.) The force of the iconic dead body is that it knows—at the very least, it has a strong intimation of—its own spectacularity. Mamie Till Bradley understood this when she insisted on an open casket in September 1955 for the mutilated body of her dead son. Burying the body in a closed casket, a private cremation, cannot hide the horrors of a young boy's body retrieved from the Tallahatchie River in 1955, but it can reveal and indict the face of Delta racism. In an open casket, where it must be viewed, looked upon, the mutilated body, especially the battered face, offers itself, first, as a spectacular reproach. Lying supine, the formal posture of the Christian dead, the dead body presents itself, with obvious effect, as an injunction against repetition: there must be no more Emmett Tills. "The murder of my son has shown me that what happens to any of us," Mamie Till Bradley reflects (in a language that would later be borrowed by King),[46] "anywhere in the world, had better be the business of us all."[47] In Mamie Till Bradley's utterance is the declaration that the barely recognizable face of Emmett Till, "Bobo" to his family and friends, must be the last face to be so mutilated. Legible in the supine black body in that Chicago casket was an inverse mirroring. In the face of the dead black boy can be discerned the faces of his murderers, Bryant and Milam, the very face of the Mississippi Delta in all its unchecked white southern violence (sovereign violence, of a sort—a violence upheld, in practice, by southern law), in all the complexity of white Mississippi poverty and its fatal commitment to the "Southern way of life."[48] Ironically, it was precisely the murder of Till that presaged the end of the worst forms of white southern violence against blacks; ironically, it was the spectacularly still, mutilated face of a teenage boy that set in motion the Freedom Riders. The body at rest activates: it not only makes political action, movement, possible; because of how it came to be at rest (first in the Tallahatchie River and then in a South Side Chicago church), it also makes political action necessary. A nation was moved to act, against its southern self, because of a black body at rest. The motion that the body at rest spurred could not be arrested by the racist history of a proud but arcane South. Such is the political effect of the body at rest.

Artest's body, of course, in no way resembles Till's, but the discourse that arose around it, because of the spectacular stillness that was the event, opens, however tenuously, into a concatenation. Artest's body on a scorer's table, where the only violence is a beer cup hurled at him or the threat of a punch, has little in common with lynched southern (and northern) bodies, bodies in coffins, buried bodies, incarcerated bodies (from the slave ships to the disproportionately large number of imprisoned African Americans), all bodies that through history—and the repetition of injustices, real or perceived, against black bodies—have acquired an eventful supplementarity of their own. What the event of Artest makes clear is that black bodies in public—and often in private—constitute, by their very presence, an event, in both Badiou's and the colloquial sense of the term, in W. H. Auden's economically eloquent phrase that "events never happen once and for all."[49] Events are, grammatically speaking, both formally punctuated and prone to taking the form of free verse—of which the bebop variety would be especially apropos—so that they always have a distinct supplementarity. The event exists beyond itself because it is repeated, in its own terms, from epoch to epoch, the past (subtraction) rearticulated in the present, the present subtracting (retracting) into the past, forming their own particular congregation. Auden's comment is, above all else, a warning. What happened once, to black bodies in this instance, can always, and does invariably always, happen again. That it happens with a difference is true, of course, but that it happens is beyond question. The event of violence opens into reconcatenations (S_1–G–S_2, followed by S_1 G S_2), that nodal point where thinking the event really commences.[50]

All this makes clear yet again how the publicly "dead," or punished, black body is simultaneously open to violation, veneration, concatenation, and unlikely congregation. In laying himself down so spectacularly, in choosing rest rather than mobility, Artest prefigured both his physical and professional vulnerability to, respectively, white race and class antipathy (the fans) and unrestricted white authority (the forebodingly named ex-lawyer Stern). The law, be it that of the NBA or the U.S. state, is always absolute for the black male body. There is, for the black body, no rest, no respite from the law; there is, furthermore, no "empty time" in the NBA. The players are, to invoke an old Fordist dictum, always on the clock. There is, finally, no time in the NBA when nothing happens. Time is also not only money, in and for the NBA; there is nothing *but* time (money, capital, infinitely generating itself)—in the eventful sense of the term—in the NBA. Time, ontologically phrased, quite simply is. For the black athletic body in the NBA, there is nothing—no rest, no alterity, no other time—outside NBA time. In its most resonant articulation, NBA time is a temporal construct unaware of its Benthamite resonances. In the enclosed space that is the NBA court, there is always the Panopticon. Everywhere, on the court and off it, there are mechanisms for surveiling all manner of transgressions, *voyou*-ishness not least among them, replete as it is with punitive possibilities, opportunities to discipline the black body. NBA law is truly sovereign in that it knows no limits, accepts no bounds. It is the law unto itself.

The "power of a truth," Badiou argues, "is that of a break."[51] By choosing to be at rest, Artest instituted a break (supineness, slowness, as interruption); he broke up the continuous temporality of NBA time. Artest's break inserted a disruptive, dissociative truth into the "uneventfulness" of NBA time. Artest's resting/Artesting, even the performance of being at rest, constituted a powerful punctuation in thinking NBA time. The event of subtraction concatenates to thinking the time of racialized American history, the actual time with which the NBA clock, so intent on providing its white audience with a culturally hip but still sufficiently sanitized black product, is out of sync. Even if the moment of being at rest constitutes only an Artestian Situation that is not properly understood, not significant enough in itself—even if it cannot be unqualifiedly named a "truth"—his subtraction marks a distinctive moment in thinking the time of race in America.

In Badiou's sense, the Artestian moment signifies as the "origin of a truth."[52] By creating an opening for, by opening up into, a potentially dissociative hermeneutic, a disjunctively synthetic truth, the body of Ron Artest at rest enables the critical devaluation of supplementarity.

In the time opened by his subtraction, because of his subtraction into spectacular stillness, there emerges a more constitutive, encompassing, congregational, complicated moment. It is a moment that enfolds within it both the event and the Situation; in Artest's case, the Situation is a singular event buried beneath the debris of supplementarity. The Artest event is that moment of temporal indeterminacy in which nothing that ever happened can ever be resolved within its own moment because it is open to every other event of violence done to African Americans. In this way, the Artest event reveals the real power of subtraction: it produces infinite addition, a force that is arguably stronger than even supplementarity. The subtraction is that event where the convoluted, reconcatenated, and repetitive nature of time means that every event, situation, and nonevent, every body and every space, demands its own moment, its own critical time. Not just once, but again and again.

2

ERIC CANTONA
The Body in Motion (Gilles Deleuze)

A reversal has happened in the movement–
time relationship; it is no longer time which
is related to movement, it is the anomalies of
movement which are dependent on time.

GILLES DELEUZE, *CINEMA 1: THE MOVEMENT-IMAGE*

In the very first line of the preface to *Cinema 1: The Movement-Image,* Gilles Deleuze sets himself a very specific task. He seeks, saliently, not to "produce a history of the cinema but to isolate certain cinematographic concepts."[1] Deleuze begins his thinking of many of these "cinematographic concepts," key among these being the movement-image (or -images, many of which he categorizes as "types") and time, through his commentaries on Henri Bergson's theses on movement. (Much of the relationship between the various types, "principally . . . the perception-image, the affection-image and the action-image," and time turns on the "representation"—direct or indirect—of time.[2]) Of course, such is the range of Deleuze's philosophical engagement with the cinema that, while he may not "produce a history of the cinema," *Cinema 1* provides an expansive critique of the work of key figures in the history of the cinema. The filmmaking of directors from Griffith to Eisenstein, from Ray to Kurosawa to Bergman, and the innovation of actor-directors Buster Keaton and Charlie Chaplin are given rich new consideration. Moreover, as Rodowick—in an impressive delineation of Deleuze's project—recognizes, *Cinema 1* is primarily a philosophical undertaking. Deleuze seeks to "write a history of 'cinematic' philosophy" by taking an "era's strategies of thinking-through, represented aesthetically in the nature of its images and signs, and render them in the form of philosophical concepts."[3] In the main, however, it is how the cinema thinks time—what time means in the cinema; the primacy of time over movement, to phrase the matter bluntly; how "relegating" movement might enable us to grasp more fully, and complexly, the workings of time—that preoccupies Deleuze.

Appropriately, then, the key conceptual contribution of *Cinema 1* is the "reversal" in—the inversion of, the reorganization of—the "movement–time relationship," "just as happened a long time ago in philosophy."[4] For Deleuze, the reversal that has occurred requires a radical reconceptualization of the cinema. That time has become independent of movement, is "no longer related to movement," means more than recognizing that the "anomalies of movement" are "dependent on time." In the course of the reversal, in Deleuze's conception, it is movement, not time, that is anomalous. It is movement that is, etymologically speaking, inconsistent with and deviating from time; movement is out of joint with time. The effect of the reversal is philosophical. Whereas time was once judged entirely as (or on) movement, as in how long it takes to get from one place to another, time has now been abstracted. Movement can no longer be said to give us our sense of time. Rather, movement takes place in time. The effect of the reversal is such that while all movement requires time, time does not depend on movement anymore. Time is the measure without measure, yet it is the measure against which movement, because it is not time, must be judged and, consequently, be found wanting. In terms of the reversal, time brings movement into itself. It is possible for time to move, chronologically, at the very least, without physical movement. Even when a body is at rest, time, colloquially speaking, moves: time succeeds itself; it registers "movement," the movement of the second hand on a clock, the changing figures on a digital watch. Even in its apparent stasis, time is moving. It is not only that movement can be said to occur in time but that there can be no movement without time; there is no movement that is not thought through time.

It is not, then, that time is no longer related to movement, in itself an impossible proposition (provocatively offered by Deleuze), but that movement is always in need of, perhaps even in search of, time. The measure of movement, distance, cannot stand against time because it is so utterly, in Deleuze's terms, related to time. It is in this way that movement is dependent on time. When theories of movement catch up with philosophy, since this happened in philosophy a "long time ago," what the reversal reveals is not—as was previously thought—the mutual dependency of time and movement but the reversal of dependency. In the reversal, theories of movement not only become (belatedly) consistent with philosophy; they become philosophical in and of themselves. Part of the process of philosophizing movement, especially as it pertains to sport, is that it compels an understanding of how (the body in) motion functions spatially. Movement cannot be conceived without the body in space—the space the body occupies, transforms, and vacates when it is either at rest or in motion. What the Deleuzian reversal makes evident is that spatiality inherently implies temporality; temporality is inferred from what is already in spatiality.

However, much as the motion of athletes, thinkable only within the space of their sport's field (or arena, or baseball diamond, or . . .) and therefore thinkable only as spatiality, is a priori subject to—related to—time, this chapter explores the possibility that there is within sport a realm in which time has essentially never been abstracted—a realm, designated in this chapter as the vertical (that is, the spatial), in which time is, arguably, not abstractable. Is it time's peculiar unabstractability in sport, its obdurate spatiality, that distinguishes sport from film (and philosophy), where the Deleuzian reversal obtains? Is the conjuncture of time and space in sport the site (or spot) from which the Deleuzian reversal is thought? Is sport always, despite its (occasional) inclining toward philosophy, destined to be always outside philosophy? Is it, to follow Deleuze's condition for the reversal, spatiality that prohibits sport's relationship to philosophy?

This chapter conceives Deleuze's reversal as the event of "temporal movement." Time is thought here as operating in terms of two sometimes complementary, sometimes contradictory coordinates: the horizontal and the vertical. The time that obtains on the field of play, the time of the game, is the horizontal. This is the time that must be understood spatially (and yet not) because it is the time that is bounded, to phrase it reductively, by space—the field of play. Horizontal time, the time of the athlete, is an instance of pure temporality—time rooted in the clock—that is effective only when abstracted time is understood in its spatiality. Vertical time is that thinking of spatiality which, in line with the Deleuzian reversal, always implies temporality. Vertical time, as will be argued here, derives from outside the delimitations of the field. In this way, vertical time is that thinking of spatiality that implies, almost unfailingly, temporality. Vertical time is the time of the spectator, the multitudinous time—unlike the singular, horizontal time, as we shall see—on which the event in this chapter turns.

Temporal movement articulates how the horizontal present temporarily, but violently, transgresses into—literally, impresses itself on—the temporal multiplicity of the vertical. When horizontal and vertical time, the time of the athlete and the time of the fan, come into conflict, nothing less than an immemorable event will follow. This was the case with, as it has now become known (appropriately, because it involves a disaffected Frenchman), *l'affaire Cantona*. The event took place when Cantona was playing for Manchester United against Crystal Palace in the English Premier League at Palace's home ground in London, Selhurst Park, on January 25, 1995. Cantona was sent off for kicking out against the Palace defender, Richard Shaw. According to Cantona, Shaw had been niggling him—engaging in behavior such as kicking him when the referee was not watching, administering the odd elbow to the ribs, occasionally tugging on his jersey—for the entire game.

An enigmatic player, much beloved by the Manchester United faithful (they crowned him "King Eric"),[5] Cantona was, writes

Simon Gardiner, "walking along the touch-line toward the dressing rooms when Matthew Simmons, a Crystal Palace supporter,
ran down to the front of the crowd and 'verbally and digitally'
abused Cantona."[6] (It is difficult to know exactly what would
constitute "digital abuse," but can we safely assume, given the
physicality and vituperation of the encounter, that it involved
Matthew Simmons's middle finger?) In response to Simmons's
abuse, a frustrated and angry Cantona launched himself into the
most historic and cinematic kung fu kick ever delivered against
a football spectator.

There are variations on precisely what Simmons said to Cantona. All the versions, however, differ only insofar as they contain
more or less xenophobic expletives: "Fucking cheating French
cunt." "Fuck off back to France, you motherfucker." Or all that
plus "French bastard" or "wanker." Cantona's own recollection
is more succinct. For him, Simmons is the "hooligan who told
me: 'French son of a whore.'"[7] Simmons, not surprisingly, has a
more innocent rhetorical rendering, a rendering that is itself not
a little *voyou*-ish: "Off you go, Cantona—it's an early bath for
you!" Cantona biographer Rob Wightman adds, crucially, that
Simmons "had run down eleven flights of steps to get to the front
by the advertising hoardings. From there he unleashed a string
of expletives at the Frenchman. Cantona flew at him, right foot
first, to deliver his soon-to-be infamous kung-fu kick."[8] (And then
there is the obvious question: would a fan really run down eleven
flights of steps to issue a mild salutation to an opposing player
who has just been thrown out of the game? Such is the defense of
the *voyou*.) The hoardings showed themselves to be but a flimsy
barrier between horizontal and vertical time, easily breached as
the protagonists were gathered together.

The red card issued by the referee (*S*: dismissing Cantona from
the game), the considerable effort expended by Simmons to issue his xenophobic invectives (*S*: bounding down eleven flights
of steps before spewing a string of expletives), and the martial
arts demonstration combine (Gather) to produce the event. The

kung fu kick is what brings all time, all the temporalities and spatialities that attend to the football match, into the event. No time is outside the event. The event gathers all time and space into itself; in the event, the reversal, as this chapter will show, must be thought again. Thinking Deleuze's reversal brings with it the opportunity to begin to think the Cantona-made event in terms of, as a first and of course by no means final gesture, Deleuze's engagement with the concepts of the cinema. What do Deleuze's coordinates mean in relation to an event in which the athlete's movement is condensed into, we might say, a single frame, the kung fu kick? Cantona's act lends itself easily to the cinematic and yet demands so much more conceptually. (The project, then, is to render Cantona's martial arts in the "form of a philosophical concept.")

Under these philosophical circumstances, it is necessary, made necessary by the player himself, to think *l'affaire Cantona* for Cantona because he refuses to do so. Unlike Zidane, who will not speak the secret, Cantona—inexplicably, implausibly—declares himself unable to explain his act. Metonymizing and thereby undermining (to the point of erasing) Simmons, Cantona offers a categorical explication, one not at all leavened by casual self-interrogation: "I'd heard him [Simmons] 50 billion times. On that day, I didn't react like I'd reacted on other occasions. Why? I've never found an answer to this myself."[9] This nonexplanation might rightly be dubbed dissembling, inflected, of course, by the disingenuousness of the *voyou*—the inability to produce an answer demonstrates the power of engagement that reveals nothing. The "answer" offered suggests contemplation—"I've never found an answer"—but, most importantly, gives away little; what it does allow Cantona to accomplish, in a *voyou*-ish way, is to record, hyperbolically, how routinely he is subjected to such abuse— "I'd heard him 50 billion times." Yet how might it be possible not to explain the act's intensity, given that he had "rammed his foot into the supporter's chest forcing him backwards. Simmons got to his feet flinging punches, but a right cross from Cantona floored him again"?[10] How does such violence not provoke an "answer," even a tentative, speculative one? The art of the *voyou* is to change the terrain of interrogation, all of it stemming from incomprehension—the inability to explain the singularity of the response, making Simmons the exceptional case of abuse, the case that is beyond the thinking of even the thoughtful, if offending, footballer. Continuing in this *voyou*-ish vein, Cantona memorably, when facing the press about the event, offered a parable in two sentences: "When the seagulls follow the trawler, it's because they think sardines will be thrown into the sea. Thank you very much." This reflection bears the hallmark of the *voyou*, the *voyou* as a figure who has thought deeply and poetically about his role in the game; this is the pronouncement of a player who has made the gnomic statement an art form (this is the form Cantona gives to the philosophical concept) and, in addition, has not let his apti-tude for brevity decenter him. In this instance, the trawler that is Cantona was doing more than putting journalists (especially those who were following him to dig up dirt on him) in their place. In reminding them they were naught but shrill seagulls waiting to catch the small fish, sardines, that were being thrown overboard, his message was unambiguous: Eric Cantona was the captain of the trawler. "Thank you." What else is there to be said after such a peremptory salutation? No less than everything. The "thank you" precludes nothing; it stands as an invitation, a forthright challenge even.

In derogating the press corps to the improbable status of sea-gulls trawling for sardines (philosophical insignificance), Cantona the *voyou* not only baited the world; he made the poetic and the gnomic unpalatable. He made it difficult, if not impossible, to ac-cept a maritime image as an explanation for immanent violence. He achieved all this, in its full complexity, by presenting the *voyou* as intellectual: the *voyou* in elliptical, allusive, and metaphoric command of language; the *voyou* in command of word games; the *voyou* playing mind games. In the guise of the *voyou*—and we can never know what articulation the *voyou* will take (an important part of its political force)—Cantona presents the deft thinking of the footballer, the footballer as *voyou* as intellectual.

Whether Cantona is being disingenuous in not proffering an answer, it is clear that, in this instance, his reluctance to publicly pronounce, to give public access to this thinking, stands as an exception to his usual grandiloquence. And the *voyou*-ish exception, we well know, inexorably draws attention to the rule. In Cantona's case, his refusal to account for his actions is uncharacteristic of a player renowned as a "philosopher," a man of reflection, among his colleagues. In the ranks of footballers, then and now, Cantona is figured as an erudite, book-loving man (a Frenchman of Italian, Sardinian, and Catalan descent who lists, among his idols, Arthur Rimbaud, for his "poetic images"[11]), given (as we have seen) to the metaphoric in his public musings, a player not afraid of controversy in his club and international career. (His career, which included stints as Manchester United and France captain, although not at the same time, was marked, and not always alternately, by brilliance and both "eventfulness" and the event.)

One of the reasons, the key one proposed by *In Motion,* that Cantona has "never found an answer" is that he is not thinking in terms of the horizontal and the vertical. *Voyou*-ish though it may be, in its own way, "I've never found an answer" is less an act of dissembling than an inability to recognize the force of temporal abstraction. Appropriately (and perhaps ironically), in Cantona's abjection (faux or not), his "I've never found the answer," there is inherent a demand for an explanation that exceeds the materiality of Selhurst Park, London, on January 25, 1995. The answer demands an abstract account, one that should not be beyond the philosopher, that is, beyond Cantona the footballer, who gives form to philosophical concepts, Cantona the philosopher, who was once a footballer and subsequently transformed himself into an actor—after which he became a football coach. (Cantona's other idols include the American actors Marlon Brando and Mickey Rourke as well as one of the iconic figures of the tragic underside of 1960s U.S. culture, the Doors front man Jim Morrison.) In positing the event as irresolvable, beyond his powers of (*voyou*-ish) interrogation, there is nothing left to do but reverse the situation and think Cantona's answer.

Because of the event's idiomatic capacity to take the coordinates into itself (gathering), the reversal itself is subject to reconsideration. In the space between the playing field and the stands, the time of the player and the time of the spectator, in the time that was—and was not—outside game time, the horizontal and the vertical come into conflict, literally, in the body of the player (Cantona) kung fu kicking the fan (Simmons). The event reveals, above all else, that game time belongs, if time can be said, in any way, to be possessed by either the horizontal or the vertical—as much to the fan as to the player, if not more so—to Simmons *and* to Cantona. The event reverses temporal expectation because, within this idiom, it is presumed that time belongs to the player, that is, to the game—to the players and the officials, not to the spectators. Is the event what must inevitably happen when time is not fully abstracted? Can the event be thought as anything other than an abstraction? Is the event of the horizontal conflicting with the vertical the effect of full abstraction, that which Cantona will not contemplate, revealing itself as an impossibility?

TIME AND SPORT

As the Cantona event makes clear, few practices lend themselves as readily to thinking the relationship between time and movement as sport. (Obviously, film would be another such practice.) That is because sport, more than almost any organized social activity, foregrounds the dependence—the relatedness, if you will—of time and movement; in sport, time and movement are revealed to be constitutive of each other. (As a consequence, of course, the philosophical, conceptual effects of the Deleuzian reversal will have a greater impact in sport than in almost any other field.) In fact, it could be said that in sport, movement has no meaning without time. The majority of sports are defined by time; it is time that provides sport with finitude ("meaning") and, therefore, its primary structure—the number of days set aside for an international cricket match (five); the number of seconds, right down to the nanosecond, it takes sprinters to finish the hundred-meter dash or middle-distance runners to finish the mile or marathoners the twenty-six-plus miles in their event.

In track events, especially, athletes are competing as much against the clock as against each other. (Of course, in the hundred- or two-hundred-meter sprint, time and space are mutually implicated—the event measures how quickly the athlete can cover space—but time, as in the most precise measurement of time, 9.83 seconds, say, is privileged. The distance is at once presumed to be the measure against which the athlete is competing, and not. What matters, finally, is how quickly the distance can be completed, hence the priority given to "9.83." Even in those professional sports not confined by temporality, such as baseball, spectators, commentators, and sponsors are keenly aware of time—of how long it takes to complete a nine-inning game in MLB; anything in excess of three or three and a half hours is a cause for concern, even consternation. Pitchers are urged, by managers, teammates, and commentators (in their address to fans), to "work quickly on the mound." Working quickly, so the governing logic goes, keeps the defense (the infield particularly) on its toes, alert, ready to make plays—ready, as it were, to come to the pitcher's assistance, helping him to register outs. Pitchers who "work deliberately" are criticized for "taking their defense out of the game." Pitchers who do not work quickly are, in Deleuze's terms, "anomalous" with their infield, out of rhythm with their teammates. Their nonsynchronicity makes these pitchers (almost) a liability to their teams.

However, within the temporal logic of professional sport, there is more than one time in play. First, there is sport's time, the actual chronological time of the game. This is a time of which the players are intensely aware. Players are expected to know how much time is left in the game; they must know how to save time if they are losing—that is, they must know how to stop the clock from running down; they must know how to preserve—and conserve—the time of competition so as to keep alive any prospect of winning; time must kept, preserved, protected against its own (inevitable) expiration; time must be saved, conserved, as though it were in itself holy. It is because of the sovereignty of time, because it alone determines the beginning and end of the game (time is, in this sense, fateful, because its expiration brings with it victory or defeat), that players must understand how to extend the game. Players must know how to make time last as long as possible to maximize the opportunity for a comeback (this applies, of course, to players on the losing side); the players are thus, to invoke an old sport truism, competing as much against their opponents as against the clock.

When a team is winning, its members must know how to run out the clock: to empty the clock of time, to terminate—one might even say eliminate—the time of the game. The very phrase "run out the clock" is un-self-consciously flush with a necropolitics of time—to end the game, to bring the game to its death, to "kill time," and not in an idiomatically idle way. (Here to "kill time" means to manage time to your advantage, to reduce the amount of time left for the opposition to secure a victory.) Running out the clock calls for nothing less than draining away the life of the game; the game is over when there is no more time left on the clock. No wonder, then, that athletes speak of the need, when they are ahead, to shorten the game, sport's parlance for making the game go more quickly, contracting it, constricting it to nothing. But not, of course, to nothingness, because there will always be the indelible mark of time on the game's outcome. Like the event, the result—victory, defeat, or a draw (a tie, in American sportspeak)—enjoys infinite duration. These phrases, in their many conjugations, express the desire for the death of game time that, for winners, symbolizes a victory over the opponent and, impossibly, time itself. The implication of the phrases "run out the clock" and "extend the game" (both of which are verbose exhortations, hyperbolic iterations that mean so little outside sport and yet, of course, everything in sport, so much so that it might not be proper even to name them hyperbole) is that, metaphorically and literally, real time can be either accelerated or slowed down to secure a victory. Or players on the winning side must understand how to run down the clock, articulating a desire to grind game time down to nothing—to eradicate, as quickly as possible, the game time that remains. Little surprise, then, that coaches and players preach the value of grinding out a victory.

Grinding out a victory means more than working hard, demonstrating great application, concentration, and attention to detail, to secure a win. At the core of the phrase is a guttural determination, derived from the verb *grinding* (a harsh enough word given added ferocity in this context), that shows how the players understand the importance of eliminating obstacles—be they one's opponents, their strategies, or just, with every play, erasing game time. It is grinding the game down to nothing (the ecritural nub, to coin a phrase, that is the written result) so that when the clock says 0:00, the win is the reward for having, as it were, overcome (game) time, for having liquidated the clock (of the game). Tomorrow, maybe a few days hence, or next week, the game clock will, of course, be resuscitated, will once again be the most formidable and implacable opponent the player must face. As long as there is the game, there can be no end to game time. The time of the game (can) end(s), but game time has—can have—no end. Game time is infinite, as infinite, as immeasurable, as sovereign, as time itself. For some fans, as for the players, the sovereignty of game time is absolute. Before the game, for the duration of the game, and for an indeterminate amount of time after the game (be it a victory or a defeat), game time is the only time that matters. It is, for the fan and the player, the only proper measurement of time.

Game time constitutes official time. It is the time, horizontal time, that is legislated and overseen by the referees and their assistants. (This is the time kept by officials; this is the only time available to the officials; for them it is the only time that counts.) Sport, however, is also a continuous-interrupted time: during the game, in the time of the game, time runs until it is temporarily stopped or game time is speculatively (that is, inaccurately but unfailingly) supplemented by the officials. In time-governed American sports, basketball and football and ice hockey, the game clock literally stops: game time is suspended, exactly, down to the second decimal; in football, the time consumed by injuries or substitutions or other stoppages is added on at the end of the regulation forty-five-minute halves; there is "extra time"—"time added on" (how does one add to time, which is infinite?) to ensure a full forty-five-minute duration of movement, of action. Extra time, also known as injury time, compensates for the time lost through inaction—especially substitutions and, as just mentioned, injuries.[12] Sport's time, in other words, must be completely fulfilled, by movement, down to the very last fraction of a second: approximately, in the case of football, and absolutely, down to the second decimal, in basketball. In fact, so much of the drama of sport derives from the battle against time—the last-second buzzer-beater in basketball, the spectacular goal right at the end of regulation or just as injury time is about to expire. Sport's time is, in this sense, faux apocalyptic: it is presented as a struggle against, if not the end of the end, then certainly against game time ending—a struggle against the irrefutable finality of game time; "time has expired," the phrase goes. The time of the game has met its temporal death. Game time has been killed.

Second, there is the time of the spectator, vertical time. This is a dependent-independent time: spectators derive their sense of time from game time but also possess an additional time, a time simultaneously anterior and successive to game time—postgame time, that time into which all thinking of the game is, inexorably, collapsed, that time when the game is, as it were, lived and relived again. And again: the afterlife of game time extends the sovereignty of game time far in excess of the time of the game. (This is time made interior, time as belonging properly inside the spectator's thinking, time living in the spectator's head.) This is a time rooted in the history of spectatorship, in the history of the fan's relationship to the club, a relationship characterized by and founded on movement, affect, pathology (more properly known as love), and history. In exceptional circumstances, such as when players emerge from the ranks of the fans of their hometown—or favorite—club, they share this sense of historical time with the fans. However, even in these cases, during the game, the players are subject(ed) to official time even as their performances might be, in part, motivated by and grounded in the historical time of the fans—the time of love, the time made, and only conceivable, because of love. For the fans, time is determined by the movement—or stasis—of the players on the field, by the movement of time (which applies not only to the game at hand but to the larger temporal sweep, meaning that players come and go), all of which allows for the sedimentation of history within the particular temporality of the fans. (The fans, of course, remain; they remain true to their club.) There is, then, always, before, during, and after the game, the thinking of movement as, to phrase it awkwardly, the time of space—time is always implicated in space. All movement, for the fan and the player, takes place in time, is only possible because of time.

And yet the site of history, its breeding ground, its shrine, is often entirely dependent on location: the space of the stadium—or, in other cases, a particular stand, such as the Kop End of Liverpool Football Club's famed Anfield Stadium. In the Kop, space is time, which is to say, the Kop End is the repository of all of Liverpool Football Club's history. That is, the club's entire history, its time, is unthinkable outside—certainly without—the Kop. The Kop is where all of Liverpool's victories, defeats, tragedies, all of Liverpool's time, is deposited and enriched in song, kept alive by swaying, red-clad bodies, moving in unison. "You'll Never Walk Alone," the club's anthem, is an absolute promise to the players (guaranteed support from the Kop End), to the club itself; it is also, of course, the fans' expression of fealty to each other: we walk together, through time, up and down these aisles, never alone. In the Kop End, time and space are one, the vertical and horizontal, movement and game time, felicitously bound by love. The *cules* (literally translates as "half-asses," the fans' rear ends exposed), rabid fans of FC Barcelona who wave the *senyeras* in Camp Nou, or the partisans of Boca Juniors who pile into La Bombanera in Buenos Aires to cheer on their team, provide other examples of such love and the peculiar vulnerability of the Deleuzian reversal.

Animus, passion, storied rivalries (between, say, teams in the same city or region; teams that have a history of cultural or political conflict), xenophobia, love, racism, wit and humor, intolerance, fanaticism, and commitment are all archived in the ontological presence of the fan. Out of this mode of fandom, history is constituted. The fan's time is, for this reason, a temporality that makes possible idiosyncratic associations; the resilience and strength of these (historic) associations enable the fan to withstand the political pressure of contradictions. The most blatant example of this phenomenon in European football occurs around race and partisanship—passionate fandom. Fans will tolerate, even adore and love, a black player on their team, while shouting racist epithets at opposing black players, either entirely unaware of or willing to live with the contradiction. Or fans of one club will jeer a player of an opposing club but support him when he plays for their national team.

Because of its architectural structure, the fan's vertical time does not (necessarily) follow chronology. The fan's time is, one might say, postmodern in its flows—arbitrary, random, and occasionally even chaotic, allowing the fan to make associations through an inscrutable, idiosyncratically sustainable logic. The fan's time is idiomatic: it speaks, and is true to, its own language. Vertical time contains a logic that makes possible the forging connections across, within, and against historical moments. What marks the verticality of sport's time is, arguably more than anything else, that it constitutes a realm in which time has not been—can never be—fully abstracted. In much the same way, fans from different sections of the stadium—which contains opposing fans, so that there is more than one vertical temporality in motion, at play, in the stands—can echo, contradict, come into conflict with, or complement each other. The verticality of sport's time reveals the unexpected tenuousness of the Deleuzian reversal. In the sport's event, the relation between time and space demands a thinking beyond Deleuze—or a thinking with Deleuze against his philosophical expectations and his cinematic conceptions (Deleuze, as it were, gathered into verticality, against his will, we presume). These coordinates, just now reorganized by Deleuze, demonstrate themselves to be, as in the case of the Liverpool fans, not so much reversed as reversible. Against philosophical expectation, the Deleuzian reversal is shown never to walk alone: it is always, in sport, in the metaphorical presence of, we might say, the Kop or Matthew Simmons and the crowd at Selhurst Park. The reversal and the reversible are philosophical coordinates related in and by the sport's event.

THE VERTICAL AND THE HORIZONTAL

Vertical time is a designation congruent with the spatial relation of the fan to the playing field—or the court, as in Ron Artest's case. The verticality of the stands, that intensely historic experience of being enclosed within the same physical site, of being connected to and yet separated from other partisans, of at once ascending outward from and inclining toward the playing field, metaphorizes the time of the fan. This is how Matthew Simmons, the Koppites, and the *cules* live their fandom. It is not simply that the fans and the players, within the same venue, occupy a different spatiality but that they inhabit distinct, contiguous temporalities: the fans are in close proximity to the time of the game but not actually in it. As player and fan, respectively, Cantona and Simmons can never live the same time, except, of course, in the event. Vertical time is not coterminous with game time, although the players can be encouraged or deflated by articulations—the supportive shouts, the derisive jeers—that emerge from the time that literally surrounds them. (Vertical time encloses or encases the players. This is the time from which neither Cantona nor Shaw can hide. Yet it is the time into which they dare not intrude for fear of the impermissible: a confrontation with a fan—the event.) This contiguous time is one that the players are as much captive to as their actions can direct. The fans' temporality is, in these ways, often inflected and determined by, as well as subject to, developments within the game.

If, as Deleuze argues, movement marks the moment of the present, then the fan's time gathers into itself, present, past, and future, in a not necessarily chronological fashion. Vertical time runs up and down, left and right, backward and forward; it even crisscrosses itself so that past (the history of the club, the veneration of certain iconic players), present (the state of the club, subject to praise or vilification), and future (the fans' ambitions for or fears about the fate of the club) all form part of a fluid, temporally distinct narrative. A current player's movement in time, his facility with the ball, his skill, or his physical prowess, could be so effective or artistic as to evoke memories of a past hero or so inept as to provoke calls for a replacement. The fans thus have their own anterior—the present—time that precedes the players and a posterior time that will succeed the current players. The afterlife of the heroic or despised player is made in the unforgettable, infinite vertical; the infinite vertical is made, on the stand that is the Kop, in the game at hand, derived from a season long gone, preserved, ruthlessly, relentlessly, for the felicitous (there can be little doubt that in the life of the fan, this is the correct adjective) vertical. The fan forgets nothing because everything matters, everything belongs to its own time; all things—the history of the horizontal not least of all—are vigorously present in the vertical, animated, given life after life, by the time of the vertical. The players come and will, more likely than not, go. Only the fans, as the constitutive political body, remain. They are the makers and custodians of vertical time. In them all time is, at all times, resonantly present—dispersed across and among them. As much as vertical time can be abstracted from the fan, that is, thought as his time, it can never be extracted—that is, expropri-ated (*Enteignis,* in its first Heideggerian sense)—from the fan.

It is for this reason that vertical and horizontal time retain, for all their proximity, a combustible relationship—they are "mutu-ally sovereign," to phrase it awkwardly. (Perhaps it is only out of a conflict between the mutually sovereign that the event can emerge.) If the fans are forever embedded in and the guardians of the vertical, the players—without whom this relationship would be, of course, impossible—are also presumed to represent (only) the players in the club's immediate ontology. The players are the club's physical embodiment on the field; the fans are its historic ontology. The fans constitute the infinite vertical: they are forever, with accommodations for conjunctural adjustments. Out of their love, because of their felicity, they are able to attune themselves to the demands of and shifts in their context. The players are, for this reason, the incarnation of Deleuzian movement. In their spa-tiality, they give shape to the (time of) the club's passing present. The players are the ones who are currently moving on the field, and in that movement, there is also their passing into history, the limits of the present that opens simultaneously into the future and provides an insight—a way of looking into, at—the past.

In horizontalness, the players' temporality is synchronized with game time; theirs is a chronological game time, a time that coincides with the continuous-interrupted ticking of the game clock. As opposed to the complicated, variegated verticality of the fan's temporality, the players' horizontal time might be de-scribed as flat, a temporality lacking the many dimensionalities of verticality. Paradoxically, then, even though Cantona and his colleagues inhabit a privileged time (because it constitutes the spectacle, the visual focus of both players and spectators), it is nevertheless a circumscribed time. The players are required to stay within the markings on the football ground, the lines on the basketball court. The players reach into the time of the fans through their performance (or lack thereof), of course, and they address the fans with their salutes after goals have been scored;

yet the wild celebration that seems always to begin in the direction of the fans finds its fullest articulation when the players mob each other. They might turn again to the fans at the celebration's end, but the body of joy is confined to the privileged. (Celebrating joy is the privilege of the privileged.) Whatever the vacillations between the exclusivity and inclusivity of their joy, however, the players have a deep desire to be acknowledged by the fans, to be directly and metonymically addressed by those in the stands. Cantona is happy to admit this: "We footballers are a particular breed. We need to hear the roar of the crowd in a football stadium. The more noise there is, the better we feel."[13] The players need to have their privileged status recognized; they want to be overwhelmed by the love and adoration only the fans can give. They want to be the object of the roar, and they want to be, for the briefest moment (in the occasion of ecstasy), subsumed by it; taken up, metaphorically and in rare instances literally, into the crowd; bathed, literally, in the roar of the crowd.

It is, however, not only in the event but (almost) without interruption that the fans address the players directly, even, or especially, it must be said, in their terrified (are we going to lose?), traumatic (the pain of defeat), or joyous silence (what a glorious, satisfying victory). The discrepancy between these modes of address constitutes, in itself, a political reversal. The ontological might speak for the vertical, but only the vertical can speak to the horizontal. In the temporal relations between the horizontal and the vertical (which derive, of course, from their affective relations), only the vertical is never silent.

Because there is no posteriority to the players' temporality that does not abstract itself through the vertical, the players' is a time that always verges on the terminal. Or, in the colloquial, the players' time is almost always on the cusp of being up. Reductively phrased, the players always stand perilously close to being eradicated from, written out of, their own (immediate) ontology; the player can always be transposed from immediate ontology into historic ontology, from the movement of the present to the static invocation in the future, which marks them as belonging to the fans' past. Cantona, a man of many interests, warns his colleagues who "have only one passion in life . . . when they no longer play football, they no longer do anything, they no longer exist. . . . Too many players think they are eternal."[14] The fans, Cantona knows, will not sing your name forever. The fans alone decide who belongs to the ranks of the eternal; the fans, it seems, more than the player himself, decide whether the player continues to exist. The player's desire to be eternal, to belong to time without end, to ascend into the most vertical of vertical times (to become a deity to the fans), is not only dependent; it also reveals how the vertical, in the end (at the end of a career, especially), triumphs over the horizontal.

It is in the moment after a game, when the roar of the crowd has faded (if it has not already entirely vanished), that the force of the horizontal–vertical reversal is felt most acutely. In that moment, the reversal is complete. Only the vertical can interpellate the horizontal into the eternal by singing his name, long after he is gone, long after he has stopped playing. That is the only way to gain entry into the eternal: through the vertical. Every player fears that he will not be granted admission into the eternal. Every player fears that his name will have passed, that the roar will now honor another name, because his name never passed properly from the horizontal into the vertical—his name, he, never transcended the restrictions of game time. Girding the desire for adoration, Cantona knows, is an overwhelming fear: how long before no one chants the name of the self anymore?

The time of a sport's event, emerging out of that moment when the proximity of the vertical to the horizontal produces a/(n inevitable) collision, can never take place in homogeneous time. In sport, the event is always an articulation of temporal heterogeneity. The event marks the contiguity of horizontal and vertical time, the time that is always potentially fraught, freighted with history—that time which is spectered by the prospect of violence, an engagement between the palimpsestic (postmodernist) temporalities of the fan and the unidimensional temporality of the players. (One would hesitate to designate the players' time Taylorist, because such is the nature of football, except for extreme versions of the game, that it presents the participants with a range of tasks that cannot be performed mechanistically. There is, however, something profoundly specialized—they are specialists of a very particular order—about the players' time.)

However, because of the proximity of the fans' time to the players' time, it is necessary to recognize the precarious absoluteness—the only discourse that can produce the event—of these two temporalities. First, it is necessary to understand that where one time ends, the other begins: at the official markings, the lines that demarcate the boundaries of the field, horizontal time terminates. And then, at the limit of the game, normally only a few meters removed from the stands, vertical time commences. That space, between the white lines (the outer limit of the players' time) and the advertising hoardings that Cantona scaled, constitutes a time that is between times but is also, simultaneously, the time of conflict, conjugation, and conjuration (the place of solemn entreaty, where players and coaches openly ask for the fans' support, the place to think about the time between the horizontal and the vertical). It is in this space, this time that has no proper temporal marking yet is crowded in on by the two times of the game, that translation takes place. The translation of one time into another, as in those moments when fans yell at, make derisive comments about, players, or when fans symbolically join the players in joyful celebration at a crucial goal or victory (reaching, hands outstretched, over the hoardings, to the players). Love, fulfilled; love, the sharing between times that now, momentarily, complement each other; openly acknowledging their love for each other. The time between that is never a time unto itself allows for the extension of one time, horizontal, and the potential penetration by another, vertical.

However, for all their difference, there is also a close link—an approximation—between the vertical and the horizontal. These times also sometimes resemble each other, have the potential to become each other; in moments of excessive affect, great triumphs, tragic, painful defeats, they can be subsumed into each other and can achieve, because of joy or violence, a terrible singularity. The event constitutes, as Yeats might have it, a "terrible beauty," full of promise, full of portent. In this moment, anything could be born. Terrible beauty is, variously, that moment of the storming of the pitch, the players saluting the fans, shaking hands with fans, both fans and players at the edge of their own temporalities. In this terrible moment, players and fans are at once in time—that is, in their own time—and on the very precipice of being out of time: of transgressing, of ultimate risk, either by accident or design, in the passion of the moment, producing a temporal homogeneity (being in sync, the two times synchronized) where heterogeneity is the normal order of temporal business. More precisely, the two temporalities can be consolidated in a single movement; each can inhabit the time of the contiguous other. The moment of the celebration or the conflagration produces, to invoke Deleuze, the relational interrogative: "When a relation terminates or changes, what happens to its terms?"[15] What happens when the time of the horizontal moves into the time of the vertical? What happens when a player or a fan acts out of time—inhabits, however temporarily, the time of the other? How are the terms of the sport's event changed? What are the consequences of disrupted temporal terms?

It took eighty-eight seconds. This event began in horizontal time, with Cantona's dismissal by the referee. It extended, in a desultory way, with Cantona's slow walk toward the dressing rooms, his movement through the interstitial temporality that separates the horizontal, game time, from the vertical—Cantona striding down the tunnel, a time permitted only to those who have an official relation to the game. In entering the time be-tween—the time of conjugation, the time of conjuration made foul by the vertical expletive; what should be, properly speaking, the time of thought—the event was born in its encounter with

Simmons's invective. The culmination was, as we well know, Cantona's charge, right foot first, into vertical time. In that short sequence, less than a minute and a half, the event not only disrupted the official relations between vertical and horizontal time but also revealed how, in a state of pure violence, sport's time opens into multiple temporalities—how sport's time is always in potential conflict with other, contiguous times.

The event, following Foucault's critique of "institutions, practices, and discourses," is what we must expect.[16] And yet, as is always the case with Foucault's thinking on structures, a certain precariousness always obtains with institutions: "a sort of general feeling that the ground was crumbling beneath our feet, especially in places where it seemed most familiar, most solid, and closest [nearest] to us, to our bodies, to our everyday gestures."[17] With this sort of general feeling, what is one to expect from Cantona, a player who, at Selhurst Park, was being sent off for the fifth time in three years? A player who had "also collected sixteen cautions in that same period"?[18] What is one to expect from a fan such as Simmons who, as irony would have it, was an amateur football referee? More importantly, however, Simmons was a fan with a criminal record and, saliently, a "BNP [British National Party] and National Front [NF] sympathizer."[19] The event is most imminent, most immanent, when the "ground is crumbling beneath our feet," when "what is most familiar" ("50 billion times," in Cantona's calculation) produces what, "to our bodies," is entirely unexpected. In the "everyday gesture," the capacity for violence is unspeakable, the familiar is unknown, and the sports body (that of both the player and the fan)—in this time that belongs to neither, this time that is outside time, this time that reveals the violent propensities inside, at the very heart of time, as it were—is shown to know a time that is only properly articulable in, or, more specifically, as, the event. It is in this way that Foucault's caution is instructive. Even if we can only know the event in its supplementarity, it remains disconcerting how it emanates from that which is closest to us (fandom, playing the game, being dismissed from the field). The event, one is almost tempted to say, is never more true to itself than when it is immersed in, and because of this arises out of, its own idiom. In this way, the event is best understood as idiomatic.

"Society Must Be Defended" highlights, read in light of the event at Selhurst Park, Foucault's insight about how eminently prepared our bodies are to produce the event (frighteningly so, in the case of Cantona and Simmons: the impetuous, too often ill-disciplined Cantona; Simmons, the right-wing political sympathizer with a criminal record of acting against foreigners). In light of this, how could we not know that our everyday gestures are the repository of an event-producing action? That our bodies, our everyday actions, are but a situation away from the event?

L'affaire Cantona demonstrates the radical discontinuity between vertical and horizontal time, the difficult link between the two that sometimes makes it impossible to conceal their differences. It is for this reason that, even though the player and the fan live, literally, in different times, there is no time that does not also have its own putative outside, its exteriority that simultaneously conceals an interiority: the time of the player lives inside the vertical spatiality of the fan; horizontal time is subsumed into vertical time (in the Badiouean sense, vertical time subtracts from horizontal time). Moreover, within sport, all time is violence; all time is potentially the time of violence because violence is always precariously, incendiarily, idiomatically, and insistently present in both horizontal and vertical time. Although the vertical and the horizontal contain, for explicable historical reasons, different kinds of violence, it is in the confrontation of the temporalities that a deeper, more explosive violence resides. The violence of the vertical is rooted in the intense verbal and physical nature of life in the stands, the undercurrent of violence that is inherent to the partisanship of sport. To be for (your team) is, perforce, also to be against (your opponents—today, tomorrow, always), is to always be for violence.

AGAINST FRANCE

The origin of the transgressive athletic movement in and against sport's time is the political. There is, among others, the politics of the player responding to the abusive or offensive fan; the player refusing the temporal limitations of the horizontal—the restraints on horizontal action that are represented by the markings on the pitch. Or, in the vertical, the fan taking offense at the player's behavior or speech, being irked by the player's gesture. Finally, however, the political stands as the decision to act in another time—to act in the time of the other. In this instance, Cantona acted in vertical time when he took offense at the xenophobic expletives hurled at him by a fan celebrating, to put the matter mildly, his dismissal by the referee. The player's transgression on the playing field has, with a single articulation (or, more precisely, a slew of attacks), revealed the precariousness of the divide between horizontal and vertical time: the thin strip of time between the temporalities is not enough to keep them apart. Because the fans are, in Jacques Derrida's terms, the "guardians" of the archive,[20] the keepers of "transgenerational heritage" and "transgenerational memory,"[21] it is in the vertical time of the Cantona event that historical animus not only resides but can also be most easily reanimated. However, as the event of Zidane shows (as discussed in the next chapter), it can as easily be encountered in horizontal time.

It is in this way that Matthew Simmons, British nationalist (of the BNP and NF variety) in the most extreme sense of the term, comes into his own as the figure who initiated the second Situation (the first was Cantona's dismissal) that gathered the event into itself. In Simmons's vituperation, there can be located, critics such as Wightman, Auclair, and David Meek agree, an antipathy to Cantona that exceeds the normal hostility fans of one team might harbor for an opposing player. According to Meek, "there was an element of racism there."[22] "Some," Meek goes on to say, "wanted him banned from the country, sent home to France in disgrace, suspended indefinitely from English football."[23] What nationalist demons did Simmons's actions unleash? English nationalist demons that had, at best, lain dormant, demons never threatened with elimination.

How is it that a twenty-year-old self-employed glazier, native of Thornton Heath, Surrey, can unleash such visceral dislike for a French player who, as irony would have it, professed such great love for English football culture and England itself? Was Simmons, a far cry from the model citizen, simply tapping into that supposed historic Anglo dislike for the French? Was Cantona so widely despised? How did Cantona come to stand as the very incarnation of offensive difference? Cantona speaks so lyrically, and with such admiration, for local British football passion, about scoring his first goal for Leeds United (the English club for which he played before joining Manchester United) against Luton Town at Elland Road, Leeds's home ground:

> At the exact moment when the ball went into the net, thousands of supporters behind the goal seemed to plunge toward the turf.
>
> This is an image which only British football is capable of giving. Here it's like a cry which rattles a cathedral. Whether you are having a good or a bad match, the public will sing profound and grave songs and then, when the ball hits the back of the net, thousands of voices sing at the same instant with their arms outstretched. It's pure ecstasy.[24]

This kind of "pure ecstasy," Cantona is at pains to say (in a range of places, in varied articulations), is not native to the game in France, the country from which had fled, more or less in disgrace, leaving a trail of footballing misadventures behind him: moderate success at Auxerre; returning home to play unsuccessfully for his local club, Olympique Marseilles; representing and even captaining France but, in the main, adrift in his native land, flitting among Marseille, Bourdeaux, Montpellier, Nîmes, Auxerre, Martigues,

Marseille. In England, especially at Manchester United, he (finally) proclaimed himself at home: "It's the club that has given me the greatest possibility for living, for feeling alive."[25] How could he not feel alive when, at Elland Road, as at Old Trafford, Manchester United's stadium, "thousands of voices sing at the same instant with their arms outstretched"? Nowhere, for Cantona, is his responsibility to the club more important than in his relationship with the fans: "As far as I'm concerned, it's like belonging to a big family."[26] How does a player who finds love in Leeds (and anger, for leaving the club) and Manchester provoke xenophobia from a fan and condemnation from the media?

In *The Meaning of Cantona: Meditations on Life, Art, and Perfectly Weighted Balls,* a series of "imagined conversations and biographical constructs," Terence Blacker and William Donaldson offer a poetic—and parodic—insight into Cantona's relationship with England: "It is one of the Englishman's greatest strengths that he can appropriate the foreign and believe that it is immeasurably improved."[27] It is one of Cantona's greatest strengths that, in signal ways, he forswore France and believed himself immeasurably improved by England—by the intense club rivalries, by the "cry that rattles like a cathedral," by the soul-sacrificing love of the game. It was precisely Cantona's foreignness that made him love England, that so immeasurably improved, first, Leeds United, and then their Manchester cousins. How is it that the event can reverse, as it were, a player's imagined relationship with his adopted home? How is it that the event can give Cantona's foreignness back to him? How is it that that event stripped him of his love for England, denied him that love? Denied him his belonging in this big family? His big family? Such is the paradox, Blacker and Donaldson argue, of Cantona: "He is a Frenchman, yet his favourite meal is tripe and onions at the Rat and Carrot, Wigan."[28] Who can deprive a Frenchman of his tripe and onions, that working-class English fare? Who can deprive a man of tripe and onions his place in English football? (Here we encounter the *voyou* in all its complication, starring simultaneously as working-class hero—football deity, connoisseur of local fare—and antihero, a figure who is no stranger to clashes with the authorities.)

Matthew Simmons. It is through Simmons that Cantona, the iconoclastic (or "arrogant," his detractors might prefer) Frenchman, can be othered. It is in vertical time that the player's falling foul of the law can be rapidly and vituperatively transformed into an act of vengeful xenophobia. In naming Cantona "French," not a Manchester United player, Simmons reveals how his movement (his present)—from his seat eleven rows removed—is motivated not by antipathy toward an English club but by its Francophone ontologization—that is, by the political. The event gathers all time—old historic national enmities—unto itself. The event is (of) infinite duration. It might have been an omission, not naming Cantona a United player, or a slip, or not; but in every way, the national designation, especially for a fan who sympathizes with the National Front, is critical. It is itself a statement of denationalizing, or deracinating, intent: England is not, in Simmons's view, whatever Cantona might conceive (however much his relationship to Manchester United, their fans, and England grounds him in this nation that is not his), the adopted country of the Frenchman's political imagination. Among Simmons, the media, and the French football authorities ("There was no talk of a disciplinary hearing. Éric was tried, convicted, and sentenced *in absentia*"[29]), Cantona was rendered, if not professionally or physically homeless, at least without a nation within a nation he loved—from its passion for football to its humble cuisine.

At the very least, Simmons left Cantona (proud son of Caillols) without a nation he could represent. (After the Selhurst Park event, Claude Simmonnet of the French Football Federation made it clear that Cantona's days of representing France were over.) Or Simmons helped to take the native's nation, France, away from him. The paradoxical consequence of xenophobia was not to return the unwanted (by Simmons and his ilk, anyway) to his homeland but to reveal the readiness of the native's homeland (at least their football officials) to make public their rejection of him. He was not wanted any more by the football establishment in France. Ironically, (the Italian-Catalan) Cantona's iconic place on the French team would be taken by Zidane, a son of immigrants, and the immigrant who would lead France to World Cup glory in 1998, on "home" soil, no less. Of course, Zidane himself would, in the wake of his 2006 event, encounter the precariousness of his own Frenchness. Zidane would learn how he, too, could be metaphorically, and politically in some quarters, rejected by the nation he had led to triumph in both a World Cup (1998) and a European Championship (2000).

Like those who, with breathtaking speed, converted Zidane from French hero into "Arab" (or worse), Simmons wanted the Other removed. Of course, in Simmons's case, he was, literally, moved by an antagonism toward a Frenchman. Simmons was motivated by a desire not only to have Cantona excised from a stadium in London but to have the player remove himself "back to France." The red card was, in this regard, incidental (but was also the instigation that comprised a situation). It provided Simmons with nothing so much as the occasion for expelling a Frenchman from England. For good. You cannot play for Manchester United if you have been "sent back to France." England, in Simmons's logic, would be free of this Other; all other Others, one presumes, in football and all other walks of British life, would surely follow. Such is BNP logic—futile in the face of Europe's diasporic and postcolonial realities but resilient to the very end.

This entire encounter turns, quickly, on movement and temporality, on movement and immobility. It turns from the nation to deportation; it asks the nation to deport the Other. The Other possesses a particular mobility, the political origin of which can be located in the time of immobility: the suspension of the body from the time of athletic participation results in the displacement of that body to the outside, to the time and space between, by the law of the horizontal. (And, finally, of course, back outside the nation; or, as Simmons and Simmonnet, whose names have a haunting—phonetic and visual—resemblance to each other, might want it, outside the nation altogether; or expulsion from the nation, by an edict decreed, of course, in absentia. Simmons and Simmonnet, the voice of the criminal and the xenophobe, finds its echo in the voice of the other nation's football authority: the voice of the law and the transgressor of the law, cast on the same side by the law.) The referee's decision to send Cantona off rendered the player immobile—he could no longer participate in the game. Cantona's last movement after being red carded was to walk toward the tunnel; to walk away from the game; to lose his right to move within the horizontal. He was condemned to move outside it; after that, all of his movements, in the main (because dismissed, players do not, as a rule, create an event such as Cantona and Simmons did), were of no consequence to horizontal time.

For the athlete, there is no time outside movement, outside the right to mobility on the field. Time is preemptively suspended in the moment of expulsion. In the moment of being cast outside horizontal time, outside the time of the law, the athlete is particularly vulnerable to the time of the vertical, to the pernicious histories that reside, mostly residually, often latently, in the archive of the fan but are occasionally revived in the moment of expulsion from the horizontal.

Banished from the horizontal, the player allows for the phantom of the political to be called into play in the time between—in the time that is neither vertical nor horizontal, and therefore the ideal terrain for the partisan political not only to be animated into footballing life but to produce a conflict between the two contiguous temporalities. Caught between the two parallel (and then converging) times, times that, because of the situation, demand a thinking together, Cantona is situated both between and in the law of the field and the law of the state. Cantona's external movement, his movement beyond the time of the horizontal law and the time between, not only disarticulates one form of the law into another but disrupts the time without law into the time of sovereign Law. Cantona, who had, by being sent off, left an absence, a physical gap, for his teammates, extended himself into a time that was already full: his legal absence was followed by an illegal—out of time—presence. It is not simply that Cantona displaced himself from that time where, in Derrida's phrasing, "authority, social order are exercised," that time "from which order is given," but that through the event of Cantona and Simmons (though much more Cantona than Simmons), they have, together, produced (a) disorder. It is not that the time, in that well-known Shakespearean allusion, was "out of joint" but that, through the event, Cantona and Simmons "joined the contiguous times." It is because of the event, or Cantona's decision to act on Simmons—to act on what Simmons had said, what Simmons was doing to him—that disorder commences, that the law of the horizontal has to be superseded by the Law of the state.

After the incident, Manchester United "decided to suspend Eric until the end of the season and fine him two weeks' wages, which, when you include bonuses, amounted to about £20,000."[30] The English FA fined Cantona ten thousand pounds for bringing the game into disrepute and banned him for eight months, from January 25 until September 30, 2005; the French FA, with whom the frequently suspended Cantona had long had an antagonistic relationship, effectively banned him from ever again representing the French national team. As for the British state, Cantona was "charged with common assault by Norwood police in connection with the Selhurst Park incident."[31] The moment that athletic movement is the consequence of a direct response to the political is signal: this is the moment that marks the limits of the "sovereignty" of the horizontal. The political is inconceivable without the specter of sovereignty: the law is always subject to the Law. To extend the Deleuzian notion of the relational: it is not simply that the very terms are revised when a relation "terminates or changes" but that the conditions of the political are transformed: horizontal sovereignty is subjected to vertical sovereignty. Cantona was "charged with common assault and pleaded guilty."[32] His sentence was eventually commuted to 120 hours of community service, which he served by coaching kids football. Simmons, meanwhile, was "fined £500 for threatening behaviour, banned from all professional football grounds for 12 months, and sentenced to seven days in prison for contempt of court."[33]

On the playing field, the maximum movement the player is allowed is all the movement the player can achieve without transgression: all the movement that is permissible before the law intervenes—referees, security, or, in extreme instances, the police. However, when the action of the athlete disrupts into a violence outside sport's time that derives from the temporary suspension of athletic action, the out-of-time violence at once produces a conflagration between temporalities and suspends the time of the game because that time, the horizontal, has now irrupted into the vertical. When the relations between the times change, it radically alters the relation between fans and players, players and players, fans and fans. More importantly, it entirely redefines how athletic movement is understood outside—or at the very boundaries of—the horizontal. The always potentially violent combustibility of the horizontal can no longer be, pro forma, presumed to have a natural termination at the white lines; the white lines, whatever their intent, can no longer be said to mark the limits of the field. Of course, that is precisely why they must be reinforced, an act that reveals nothing so much as the violability of the white lines—of the limit itself. The limit does nothing so much as create the conditions for its (own) undoing. If the temporalities that inhere in the vertical and the horizontal have a certain natural difference, if the two seem to be separated from one other by a structural discontinuity, the event demonstrates that this no longer holds as an absolute.

The conflictual relationship of the different temporalities, their tense, sometimes antagonistic interaction, affords a particular possibility to Cantona. It was Cantona's decision, and only Cantona's decision, to act: his act made the event possible. Had he chosen to ignore Simmons as he had ignored his countless progenitors, there would have been, of course, no event. Simmons, whatever he said, whatever his sense of his ability to offend, could not have made the event. The force (or the power, we might say), of Cantona's decision, by itself (if such a compartmentalization might be, for a moment, permitted), is brought fully into view when measured against Simmons's prior anonymity. The event can, in this instance, be said both to have been made by what Simmons said and to have absolutely nothing to do with it. (After all, what Simmons said had been said to Cantona scores of times before, whereas Zidane had never, we presume, encountered anything like what his antagonist said to him.) The decision to act can only, for this reason, be described as an irrational act: committing the act that must not be committed; committing the act even though it is not permitted; knowing reason yet not following it. Reason and what we might hypostasize as "reason," like vertical and horizontal times, exist in tension with each other; they can be mutually supportive and dependent on each other, to be sure, but this can in no way disguise that these times are in a volatile relationship.

The continuous-interrupted nature of sport's time assumed, in the act of horizontal violence that was balletically vertical, the footballer lunging into the contiguous time with his martial arts performance, a violent irruptibility. When the relations between times change, everything within sports time itself is, at the very least, altered: made to understand itself as the articulation of difference. It is for this reason that Cantona's kung fu kick to the chest of Simmons, a Crystal Palace fan who had "been banned from Selhurst Park the previous season for his part in a pitch invasion during a match against Watford," is not simply about transgression or aggression.[34] Cantona's is the act of acting against the laws of temporal division. His going into the stands constitutes the act of temporal invasion and, more dangerously, temporal invalidation: acting in and against the time of the Other, the time that divides the athlete from the spectator. It is only in the time that is athletically proper to the self that the self can be itself. In horizontal time, the self can be true because the time of the law is not the time of the Law.

There is, then, in Cantona and Simmons, a self-proclaimed

"French philosopher" and a "self-employed glazier" from Surrey, an uncanny symmetry that is simultaneously asymmetrical:
neither the footballer nor the fan is able to act exclusively in his
own temporality. Both the footballer and the fan refuse, in key
moments, to be restrained by their times, and both feel compelled
to act out of time. They consider the time afforded them, as player
and fan, restrictive. They both want greater room for movement,
another time to inhabit. Their irruptive movements derive from the
same place: both of them are subjects motivated by the political,
be that a refusal to accept xenophobia or an affinity for extreme
right-wing groups. Both Cantona and Simmons are, in Derrida's
sense, political subjects plagued by "archive fever," but with very
different understandings of the archive:

> The question of the archive is not, we repeat, a question of
> the past. This is not the question of a concept dealing with
> the past which might *already* be at our disposal, *an archiv-
> able concept of the archive*. It is a question of the future, the
> question of the future itself, the question of a response, of a
> promise and of a responsibility for tomorrow.[35]

For both Cantona and Simmons, the political is understood as the
"question of a response": when the question, which takes the
form of xenophobic offense or partisan helplessness brought on
by location in the stands, is addressed to them, both the athlete
and the fan consider themselves compelled to engage it, to address
it fully and, if necessary, violently.

These are, for Cantona and Simmons, questions that come from
another time, from a time outside their own, and it is in this way
a "question of the future itself" because it will determine, this
question, how they inhabit their respective times: as the French
athlete perpetually vulnerable to abuse, especially when not protected by the law of the horizontal, or as the "proud Frenchman,"
"the first existentialist footballer," who considers himself responsible for a tomorrow, a time when the vertical will not constitute

such an existentialist threat to his sense of political self. And so Cantona, acting in another time, violently insists that the vertical might be a different time—a non- if not antixenophobic time. Cantona seeks to rearchive the vertical archive, to produce within it a different politics. Simmons, for his part, sees in Cantona the specter of a proliferating Frenchness or, more specifically, a greater number of players from Europe, Latin America, Africa, and Asia. There are more and more Others in the English Premier League, a future where his nationalist sense of self is vulnerable to the cosmopolitanness of the English game. Foreign players are lured to the league not only by the pound sterling (which makes the Premier League the richest and therefore the most attractive to players the world over) but also by the very values that Cantona lauds: the competitiveness, the intense physicality, the utter investment of the fans; the songs, songs of love and pathos, grave songs, songs of joy, all of which echo from the stands at Anfield and Old Trafford, Stamford Bridge and Elland Road. As it has turned out, Simmons saw the future: Simmons, in taking his role in the event, gave his name to the fear of a Premier League that has made English players at once a diminishing presence and, increasingly, a valuable commodity. In terms of the state, the British government has stiffened penalties for ethnic and racist abuse at English football grounds. Some of those changes were effected precisely because of what took place on January 25, 1995. Others were already in place but are now attended to more carefully because of *l'affaire Cantona*.

Neither Cantona nor Simmons, as figures of the political, could be contained by the horizontal and the vertical. Little wonder, then, that they both, in their different ways, did time (were punished by the Law), marked the time of the horizontal and the vertical, were marked by the horizontal and the vertical. Through the event, they brought starkly into view how players and fans inhabit their different, always intensely related times. The Law may punish, the sovereign might seek to impinge on the vertical and the horizontal, but the Law means little—if not nothing—in the face of the force of these temporalities. The time of the event is never, of course, autonomous, a time unto itself (unless that time is of infinite duration), but it does make clear the force of time. What the Law fears, as it rightly must, is its own limits. What the Law fears is that, for the player and the fan, time has a force—exercises a force on all the participants at a football match or a basketball game—that exceeds the Law, that goes beyond the Law's reach. Time is stronger than the Law. The Law knows this; it also knows, just as well, that it must not allow itself to know this. Like Cantona, the Law, which prides itself as, grounds itself in, reason, cannot anticipate, mediate, or eliminate hypostasized reason. The Law cannot know (because this is precisely what it fears), like Cantona (who seems to have no such fear, making him such a great threat to both his own reason and the Law), what reason (Cantona, already a precarious incarnation of the horizontal) will do in the face of hypostasized reason (Simmons).

The Law cannot fine Simmons out of existence because the vertical belongs too much, too constitutively (Cantona knows this more eloquently than most), to the horizontal. What Cantona reveals, then, is not so much that he is a bad or delinquent custodian of the horizontal as that he is its most revealing incarnation: "As far as I'm concerned, it's like belonging to a big family."[36] Cantona knows football first, if not only, as, to amend his terms, the "family of time," the family of all time. "People are sometimes surprised," he says, "that I give so much of my time to the fans." What else does the player have to give the fan, to give the game, but time? To give time to the fans is, unknowingly, to live in the time of the fans: to live in two temporalities at once and to know that, in a certain moment, there may only be one time—the time of the event.

What does the event give us, as if for the first time, but time? What does the event do but make us acquainted with time, as though we were strangers to time? What does the event make pertinent, unavoidable, pressing, as Heidegger teaches us, but a thinking of time? The event illuminates the force of time pressing

down on the player, the force of time—the game is a gift of time—
that will, in its own name, refuse, even if only for the moment that
is the event, the horizontal and the vertical. This is, more than
any other rendering of temporality, the time that Cantona gave
himself to, the time that gathered him—took him—unto itself, at
Selhurst Park, the time that was felicitous to nothing but itself.
It is impossible to love the game without first submitting, giving
the self over, to time itself. It is time that relieves Cantona of his
perplexity. When he says, "On that day, I didn't react like I'd reacted on other occasions. Why? I've never found an answer to this
myself," he allows inexplicability to overwhelm what he already
knows. The event is chance. The event is true to nothing so much
as its own idiom. In the decision to "give time to the fans," there
is, inherently, the decision to enter the time of the fans, that is,
to make time singular—to restore, we might say, time (to) itself.

3

ZINEDINE ZIDANE
Coup de Boule (Jacques Derrida)

When speaking of a voyou, one is calling to order;
one has begun to denounce a suspect, to announce
an interpellation, indeed an arrest, a convocation,
a summons, a bringing in for questioning:
the voyou must appear before the law.

JACQUES DERRIDA, *ROGUES: TWO ESSAYS ON REASON*

Because of its elusiveness, the *voyou* is understood here as the "rogue" (retaining a certain fidelity to the translation of Derrida's text), but as the "rogue" who is not beyond petty criminality (of the—bank heist—variety practiced by "Simon the Swiss" in the 1970 movie *Le Voyou* [*The Crook*]) or who is engaged in what might properly be named delinquency (arguably the best way, the most efficacious term, for keeping undetermined whether the behavior in question falls inside or outside the law—is it delinquency or in blatant violation of the law?). The *voyou,* then, is a political subject that is difficult to identify exactly, a figure capable of artful deception, of seductive trickery, and even, at times, of pure seduction. In the last instance, the *voyou* goes by that familiar and most endearing moniker, the "lovable rogue." That is why there is such a thin line between, say, a *voyou* and the wayward citizen, why it can be difficult to tell the disenfranchised citizen, *le citoyen,* apart from the illegal immigrant, *sans papier.* It is (in) the nature of the *voyou* to make it difficult to distinguish, with absolute certainty, the criminal, the "suspect," the delinquent, if you will, from those immigrants who are noncriminal, those raced bodies above questioning or outside the orbit of interrogation or "interpellation"—from the law abiding, or generally law abiding. Above all else, the indefinability (a quality not unrelated to a kind of indefatigability) of the *voyou* derives from a constitutive uncertainty: it is impossible not only to identify the *voyou* (who is the *voyou*? Is he or she a *voyou*? How can the identity of the *voyou* be determined—beyond, that is, what seems like unreasonable doubt?) but also to tell how far the law reaches into behavior: what is the reach of the law in relation to the *voyou*? The *voyou* provokes a foundational quandary for the law because it vivifies a difficult confrontation with the irascibility (the "lovable rogue") that both haunts and taunts the law at its limits, taunts the law to its limits. After all, what, if anything, can the law do to the *voyou*? What can the law not do because of the *voyou*? What is the force of law if all it can do is act with impunity against the petty criminal, if it brings its full force against marginal transgressions?

The waning minutes of the 2006 Coupe du Monde final, between France and Italy, was marked by a *voyou*-ish act. It was an act of violence, now renowned as the *coup de boule,* head butt, committed by then captain of the French team, Zinedine Zidane, in response to something that was said to him by an opposing player, Marco Materazzi. We do not know, it is important to recognize, what was said. What was said is, and remains, a secret. We do know that after Materazzi pulled Zidane's jersey in the Italian penalty area, Zidane said something when he passed Materazzi on his way out of the Italian penalty area, reportedly something about giving Materazzi his jersey when the final was over. Zidane was referencing, sarcastically, the customary act of exchange of jerseys after a big game. "Zizou," as he is more popularly known, was making the point that he did not like Materazzi's tactics, especially the Italian's aptitude for pulling opponents' jerseys when the referee wasn't looking. Zidane made his comment in situ, running away—running past, again, a not unusual practice in sport: making your point on the run, in motion; just letting your opponent know that he or she is doing something you do

not particularly like. Materazzi then responded, it has been variously claimed, by denouncing Zidane's sister as a "whore" (or
"prostitute") or calling Zizou the "son of a terrorist whore." On
hearing what was said to him (a matter on which, again, we are
not clear), Zidane turned toward Materazzi and rammed his head
into the Italian's chest. The entire exchange lasted a matter of
seconds. In this instance, the exact measure of time is that brief
instant it takes a player to pull an opponent's jersey, trade insults,
and respond with a violent act: that is, almost no time at all—not
in game time or, for that matter, "real" time. Just a few ticks of
the clock is all the time it takes to make the event—or the time it
takes for the event to make itself.

The event between Zidane and Materazzi was, in purely visual terms (the observation of the event, not its processing, not
its thinking), over before it started. It happened, initially, away
from the camera, seen only by a handful of spectators (a relatively
small number: those who were close to the action, those who were
paying especially close attention to developments on the field, or
those who were keeping a special eye on Zidane, the best player
on the field). But then the camera (which misses nothing, except
that it missed the event before making the event) re-turned and
re-created it for hundreds of millions of viewers as if it were happening then, in that very moment, before the eyes of the whole
world. The world was, literally, watching the World Cup "head"
for an (unprecedented) event.

The Coupe du Monde had already "headed" itself into the
event as, the shocked commentator said, Zidane "leaves football in
disgrace." The *coup de boule* led to Zidane's dismissal; the captain
had just played the last seconds of the final game of his storied
career. The *coup de boule,* which, momentarily, assumes the status of Situation rather than event, led to nothing less than the
unraveling of the Coupe du Monde (that rare pseudo-event that
produces the event). The turn of events was such that the event of
the 2006 World Cup was the *voyou,* Zidane and, to a lesser extent,
Materazzi (a *voyou* of a lesser order). The event of the Coupe du

Monde was the *voyou*, the final itself "merely" a Situation gathered into the event. As the commentator proclaimed, this "unsavory moment" would become, (no) pun intended, the "headline beyond the result." It is unprecedented that the winning or losing of the World Cup final should not matter. But in this Coupe du Monde, Zidane's head had, as it were, drawn a "line" under his act. The head action caused an interruption of the game that produced, as in Artest's case, an irruption, one that raised similar issues, albeit this time issues that turned on ethnicity (although ethnicity can never be fully disarticulated from race), the history of migration (the consequence of French colonialism), and religion in a post-9/11 world. Because of what irrupted from the actions of the head, Zidane's head made itself the event, overshadowing everything else, including Italy's win—a win, on penalties, that came after an absorbing but not especially attractive contest between two very different European teams. Zidane's team did their level best to play attacking football, and the Italians responded, as is their custom, with a commitment to dour, sometimes cynical defensive tactics. Fortunately, the Italians have a lyrical name for it. They call it *catenaccio*.

At the end of the regulation ninety minutes, the World Cup final was tied at 1–1, courtesy of goals, as fate would have it, by Zidane (a penalty after Materazzi had fouled Florent Malouda) and Materazzi (a header, of course). And so it continued until late in the second half of extra time. With only minutes left, Zidane picked up the ball with his gazelle-like, loping grace and danced into the Italian half before laying a pass off beautifully into space for the selfsame Malouda, one of many "players of color" on the French team; the preponderance of "players of color" in the French quad (twenty-three in total, from which the coach selects his starting eleven and seven substitutes) was much maligned by right-wing French nationalist Jean-Marie Le Pen. (Le Pen bemoaned the absence of "French," that is, white French, players.) Zidane continued his run and, eluding with nonchalance the Italian central defenders, Fabio Carnavarro and Materazzi, drifted behind his markers and headed the ball with his trademark control and power. In the Italian goal, Gianluigi ("Gigi") Buffon saved brilliantly, going high to his left and tipping the goal-bound header over the bar. Almost immediately afterward, it seemed, Materazzi felt the force of Zizou's head in a very different way.

This chapter is only in part, and then only incidentally, an attempt to understand the motivations for Zidane's head butt, only in part a thinking of the unspoken problem of race (Le Pen's "players of color," the ongoing legacy of racism in sport) and language (a presumptively private, hidden, unspeakable discourse) during a Coupe du Monde. The focus is, for this reason, on Zidane as *voyou,* supplemented and complicated by (and simultaneously juxtaposed with) Materazzi. The Italian is Zidane's foe, his nemesis, and yet the player with whom Zizou is bound in and by the event as *voyou*. This thinking of the *voyou* is then, for this very reason, a thinking of the *voyou* in its many registers. Zidane operates, to phrase the inquiry reductively, in the "major" register and Materazzi just a notch below (that is, by no means in a "minor" register).

It is alleged that Materazzi said something deeply offensive to Zizou; it was this speech act that led, the argument (justifiably) goes, directly to the *coup de boule*; up to now, years later, it is still not known what secret thing was said, from one player to another, what preceded it, how it was heard (that is, received, politically understood; what the speech act "meant"). The secret, as such, exists only between the two protagonists because it is articulated, can only be articulated, freighted with a history (such that language, only language, can bear) that exists—and has effects—well beyond the secret. This chapter thinks the impossible possibility of the event of the secret—the secret, which both is and is not, for structurally essential reasons, kept. The event of the secret constitutes a kind of unpredictable, incalculable venting of the secret: the secret that constitutes a sharing that is also an expelling, making or stating (publicly) the public fact of the secret. The event of the secret signals, at once, in juxtaposition, operating with divergent purposes, a foreclosed *voyou* relationship (Zizou and Materazzi) and a public document that envelops—inveterately draws in, gathers to itself, Situation by Situation—the monde/mondial/world. The secret is the incalculable sum of what we, spectators, officials, and players, are sure we are privy to (after all, the game, the language of the game, the very nature of the event is such that it is always presumed to be known by the public) and can never know. Who knows what happened on that Berlin evening of July 9, 2006? Who knows, beyond the restless speculation (by its very nature, speculation is restive; it cannot come to or remain, for that matter, at rest; speculation is relentlessly mobile), what happened between the brilliant, sublimely talented "boy from the banlieue," Zizou, and the Italian hard man, the defender Materazzi? Does it matter that we know? How could it not matter? Why would we not want to know what was said, what happened? Why not account "fully" for Zizou's act, the *coup de boule,* the head butt that launched a million talking heads? The head butt that reverberated into the chat rooms of the Internet, into the cafés and bars of Europe, North Africa, the world, to say nothing of the condemnation, explication, praise, and even national recuperation that followed after Zidane took his head to Materazzi's chest, leaving his tormentor flat on his back, felled by the head? On his back, the *voyou* (Materazzi) called on the law (the referee) to enact itself (by sending off Zizou, showing Zidane a red card, the law's sign for expulsion), while revealing the law's utter inadequacy: it could not pronounce on what Materazzi had said. The law, made up of words, has no means for pronouncing on what is said. Language, spoken secretly (privately, between two individuals—or any form of "closed" communication), is beyond the law. The law is powerless in relation to precisely what grounds it, what makes it up: language. The *voyou* is most *le voyou* (when it acts like a petty criminal; when it is unjust, that is, "crooked") when it says what it wants just out of earshot of the law and then calls on the law to protect it against a transgression it, the *voyou* alone, has instigated—the word, the words, Situation followed by Situation, gathered together, a synthesis at once disjunctive and utterly synchronized, that escalates the routine insult into the event. The *voyou* Materazzi who, in this instance acts in the register just below, is most effective when he says what he wants and gets the law to act to his advantage, while the law knows, beyond question, that it has been transgressed and yet stands helpless but to become an accomplice to the transgression against it.

This is the law at its most roguish—or the law as full-fledged *voyou*, because there is nothing diminutive, that is, a "little crooked," about having been exposed for its inability to uphold itself. Such is the force, the wiliness, the roguishness, of the *voyou*: it reveals the utter vulnerability of the law to the *voyou*. No one, to render this abjection of the law in the vernacular, can "play" the law like the *voyou*. The *voyou* makes the law unable to uphold its own terms, except in the most farcical way: by acting in its own name when the transgression it should have acted against is precisely the one that it is unable or, sometimes, unwilling to punish. The transgression has already happened—making Materazzi the *voyou* par excellence because he did not get caught. The *voyou* is the closest the law gets to the face of its own ineptitude, its own constitutive helplessness, its own autoimmunity. No figure of the political makes the law so vulnerable as the *voyou*—the *voyou* neutralizes the law at the very moment that the law should be acting to uphold its (own) authority.

The event of Zizou set in motion, as is the nature of the event, a world of discourses. The historicity of Zidane's act on a football field can only be properly apprehended if, as this chapter shows, the *voyou* (Zidane and Materazzi) is thought in—with, against—its political relation to the secret and the event. The relations among these concepts must be thought, to borrow from Mary Jacobus, as a "form of *désouvrement*, in Blanchot's sense—a restless un-working that refuses totalization and proceeds not by way of critique, but rather juxtaposition, divergence, and difference."[1] Figuring Zidane, the World Cup–winning (1998), European Championship–winning (2000), Champions League–winning (with Real Madrid) footballer, as a *voyou*—a term that has already been shown to refuse totalization, a term that incarnates restlessness, a term capable of working, sometimes willfully, against itself (unworking)—opens the possibility for thinking the relations among these concepts as a form of *désouvrement*. Thinking the juxtapositions, divergences, and difference(s) between Zidane and Materazzi (the *voyou* and his fellow *voyou*) and among the *voyou*, the secret and the event opens up onto an unworking of these concepts. The effect of the tensions among these concepts is not only to set them against each other, as it were, but to take each of them apart from the inside, beginning with their own detotalization. In thinking their juxtaposition, divergence, and difference, the task is set: to imagine and propose new ways in which they might be, first, put together individually, and then how to reconceive their relations with each other. To think the *voyou* on his own but never in singularity. To think the *voyou* when it is in direct conflict with the *voyou*, provoking the question of historical consequence: who is the *voyou*—Zizou? Materazzi? What possibilities open up if they are both thought as the *voyou*?

The force of the event of Zidane and Materazzi the *voyou* is that it draws us—it gathers the world—into the secret that turns, it seems, on juxtaposing the three concepts, on thinking their difference and divergence both from within themselves and through their restless cohabitation, or origination, in the *voyou*. And, in so doing, the event makes imperative and inevitable a thinking of the *voyou* from within its very self, again, that we might see the *voyou*'s opacity.

THE EVENT: ZIDANE AND MATERAZZI

Zidane moved according to his own time, in his own time, in a time he made his own. The event of Zizou and Materazzi was frozen in time. It was locked into the slowness of Zizou's motion (interrupting the motion of the game, gathering the World Cup final into the time of Zizou), Zidane moving forward, toward Materazzi, with a sureness that was directed and yet, strangely, not hurried. Throughout, Zizou's hands hung lightly at his sides, as if, in the fashion of the *voyou,* to suggest that he was acting within the broad framework of the law of football, while the intention was clearly to transgress. Zidane broke the law (he performed physical violence in response to Materazzi's rhetorical violence), but only after Materazzi had tested, with unspeakable success (what a literally subtractive practice it is, to commend a player—be that teammate or opponent—for enacting rhetorical violence against a member of the other team to have that player eliminated from the game, in a World Cup final, no less), the limit of the law.

What does the Coupe du Monde do when it stages, is upstaged by, a *coup de boule* that was orchestrated by the *voyou*? Zidane did not, as is often the case in on-field violence in football, and in sport in general, use his hands—at least gesturally. (Here we might think of the staged and, it sometimes seems, inevitable fight in professional ice hockey in the United States and Canada. In many games in the National Hockey League, would-be combatants, known as "goons" or "enforcers," on cue, drop their gloves and square off in a "fight" that can sometimes be quite violent but is often little more than two adversaries tugging at each other's jerseys; although the two players are raining punches, it looks more like they are helplessly flailing at each other.) The event in Berlin was not a matter of the usual meaningless banter or theatrical fisticuffs. Materazzi used his head (rhetorical provocation), as it were, and in response, Zizou used his (first to respond with sarcasm, then as a battering ram). Zidane used his head—a perfectly legitimate action in the game, except, of course, when the head becomes a cranial weapon—just seconds, it seems, after his head had almost won the game and a second World Cup for France. A Coupe du Monde, almost won, and then lost, in the head, with the head, because of the head.

A notoriously "restless" figure, a player of sublime, stealthy, and always precise movement (he always seemed to know the purpose and direction of his movement, as if he could see the only perfect place on the field for him to go toward). As a player whose divergence from the nationalist imaginary (as a Kabyle, a Frenchman of Berber descent) offended right-wing France (led, of course, by Le Pen), Zizou the *voyou* reveals the "restlessness"—the difficult philosophical movement that emerges from the interplay, the "juxtaposition" of self, nation, and athletic performance—that is the inevitable consequence of thinking concepts such as the rogue and the secret together. (Le Pen attacked the racially mixed team that represented France at the Coupe du Monde in Germany in 2006. This was not, Le Pen intimated, a "team of Frenchmen." The 2006 edition of Les Bleus was incommensurate with the white, racist national imaginary of Le Pen and his supporters. "Maybe," Le Pen offered, "the coach exaggerated the proportion of the players of color.")[2] Who knows where (the initial) restlessness might lead—what thinking it might produce, what paths, political or philosophical, it might open on to? What happens when "totalization," itself nothing but a deep inclination for the absolute, for encompassing everything, accounting for everything, is undone in the process of confronting its own difference?

In this regard, the only proper first response is to be overwhelmed by the event. That is a crucial feature of the event: it demands a thinking of the event on its own terms, so no existing responses, no language of sport, say, is adequate to the event of Zidane and Materazzi. For this reason, it is appropriate that not even Zidane and Materazzi, those closest to the event, those who made it, can really know the why, what, and how of the event. It is in the nature of the event that it comes about only as an unforeseeable concatenation of actions—not a neat, tidy sequence, although that is possible, but rather, as in this case, an act of provocation responded to with self-asserting language, which then produces a secret, and then, of course, violence; this form of concatenation, this mode of linking, gathering Situations together, is what leads (up) to the event: not inexorably but because of the particular set of connections (that is, politics and history).

The event is incalculable and unpredictable because it is like the tiny modulations and the "random" outcome of things on the field of play—the vision to conceive a brilliant pass, the mobility to fashion a header that seems destined to become a goal that is denied by instinctive goalkeeping. Random concatenations, Situations, produce historic effects. Had Zidane not made the pass to Malouda, had an Italian defender intercepted Zizou's or Malouda's pass, or had Zizou scored a second goal, the event might never have occurred. France would have won the Coupe du Monde, and there would have been no event. Such speculation is moot, of course, except in that it reveals how the event is the effect of the unforeseeable; the event is secretly lodged, undistinguished, unbeknownst even to itself, until it irrupts into the routine. (Because of this, of course, the event might find its articulation in the game, even a game as signal as the World Cup final, but the event neither begins nor culminates in the game.) It is for this reason that we do not, at a fundamental level, need to know the secret—what Materazzi said—to insert ourselves into the event (or the event of the secret), to stake a claim on a time that was originally not ours but was, of course, made entirely ours, because the event of the Coupe du Monde belongs, first and foremost, to the world. So it is appropriate that the world should locate itself in the time and space of the event (the event of the secret, the event that comes, as it were, out of the secret) it does not know but by which it is entirely surrounded, enveloped, intrigued, and all the while unconcerned about its own "ignorance" (the "not knowing" what was said between Zidane and Materazzi). This was an ignorance, of course, alleviated and "remedied" by the world's infinite capacity to interpret, whether through lip readers or political critique. When asked whether he had in any way used the derogation "terrorist" against Zidane, Materazzi acted every inch the *voyou*. He was, Materazzi replied, "too ignorant" to know what a "terrorist" was. The only connation of *terrorist* with which he was familiar, Materazzi went on, was the behavior of his "ten month old daughter." In this self-rendering, Materazzi is among the few members of our technologically advanced society to have successfully escaped the realities of the post-9/11 world, the world that "terror" made.

Such are the ways of Materazzi the *voyou,* such are the secrets of the *voyou,* the secret that bears directly on—because it comes out of—the event. In this regard, try as he might, Zidane cannot escape his own Kabyle naming—it is the name that makes him other, that makes him vulnerable to the possibility of discursive othering, an othering intensified by the event of 9/11 and its Islamophobic aftermath. It does not matter whether Materazzi named him as such; the resonance of Zidane's Algerian, and consequently France's imperial, past (the conflict between Europe and North Africa; the humiliation of imperial France's defeat; the conflict, given new life by 9/11, between Islam and the West) is easily animated by the event. It takes very little to speculate the politics of othering—Islamophobia, xenophobia, racism—into discursive life. The subtractive practice of the event is such that it draws the political into it; that is, every aspect of politics falls under the rubric, the authority, of the event.

Not surprisingly, then, Zidane cannot escape the public resonance of his name, "Zinedine Yazid Zidane." Zizou might think himself to be, as he has publicly said, a "non-practicing Muslim" married to a Roman Catholic Spanish-French wife, Véronique Zidane (née Fernandez Lentisco). No matter that he is the father of four sons, all of whom have obviously Christian names, of which the older two are distinctly Italian in flavor—Enzo, Luca, Théo, and Elyaz.[3] A faith may be renounced, shaken off, half-heartedly or fully rejected, but the trace of the history of the name remains inscribed on the name of the subject, inscribed through the name of subject. He is, this captain of France, icon of the republic, "Zinedine Zidane," understood to be a son of the Kabyle, one generation removed from North Africa. He is French by birth, other by political identification, made Other by the event. That other place, that place of other, that is, to paraphrase Jacques Derrida, "not my own," that condition remains, always, proximate to him.[4] "Zinedine Yazid Zidane" situates Zizou, for Le

Pen and probably also for Materazzi, outside Europe, outside the nation, outside his wife and sons, and relocates him to another time, because the secret is always marked by violence, by an act whose speaking is never fully permissible within the public and, in its "secrecy," remains as the trace that haunts the public. It is for this reason that Derrida and Heidegger would insist, each in his own way (with Derrida's invocation full of Heideggerian echoes), that every postimperial nation constitutes nothing less than a haunted dwelling,[5] a place that can only—even in the moment of the European nation's triumph (1998, 2000)—be dwelled in with difficulty—or, in Zizou's case, in a characteristic silence off the football field. This may be the enduring feature of Zidane's secret: his obdurate ability to keep so much of himself to himself. Zidane's secret is, in this way, a remarkable accomplishment, given that this (impossibly secretive) self must endure in the face of all manner of public derogation, speculation, and inquiry—and worse, of course.

As such, the event is the time of history (colonial, postcolonial, the time before and after 9/11). The event is the time that must always be anticipated and, of course, guarded against by the sovereign. As such, the event cannot, finally, be explained, not even with a full recapitulation—impossible, of course—of the temporally brief but historically extended exchange between Zidane and Materazzi. If, as Derrida argues in his critique of the United States as an *état voyou,* a "reason must be reasoned with," then the event of Zidane demands a special kind of reasoning: it must be thought, the event, the secret, as a "reason" that demands not only a considered response but a thinking that begins from the premise that, in this instance, it may be impossible to articulate the "reason" that will allow for the process of "reasoning with."[6] The reason may be in excess of what can be thought, which is precisely why it must be thought—why this "reasoning with" may have to start with a "reasoning against reason" as it is known; against how it is things stand; against "reason" as being a priori sufficient as a mode of explanation.

The event of Zidane requires a reasoning not least of all because FIFA, football's governing body, had no clue about how to respond to it. Banning Zidane for three games after he announced his retirement (where is the sanction in that?) and fining him £3,260, and banning Materazzi for two games and fining him £2,170, is hardly the required action.[7] It is hardly a disincentive to the *voyou*. All FIFA's decision does is reveal the law's inability to produce, in response to the event, a proper sanction, a sanction that could stand—that judged the history and the politics of the event—in the face of history. Furthermore, what FIFA's judgment reveals is that the law and the sovereign—narrowly conceived here, as it relates to who has dominion over the game, who has dominion over the *voyou*, all the while recognizing, of course, that *voyou* draws the issue of (state) sovereignty into thinking through sovereignty's response to the *voyou*—acknowledge in their ineffective sanction that the sovereign does not have a monopoly on violence. It follows, then, that the sovereign cannot sanction—with any integrity or real effect—the *voyou*. The sovereign can (only) make the pretence of sanctioning the *voyou*, a fact already well known to the *voyou*. Above all else, the *voyou* knows—has known throughout history—what the sovereign cannot do.

The event demands an appropriate response from the sovereign not least because the event is a dramatic rupture with the usual narratives for interpreting verbal attacks, on-field provocations (following a logic that understands the provocation, the insult, "needling," "trash talk," and so on, as endemic to the game), and physical violence on the field of play. For many, football administrators, referees, and spectators, this is all a "normal," even constitutive, part of the game. Indeed, Materazzi, as is the tendency of the *voyou*, was quick to point out that he had done nothing "unusual" in his exchange with Zidane. In effect, by insisting on the accepted nature of (the language and politics of) the secret, Materazzi was publicly staking a claim for the secret as apolitical—as that which stood outside the politics of race, gender, or ethnicity. Materazzi wanted to stand, simply, as a footballer—as a competitor who had operated within the discursive framework of the game. There is an unquestionable logic to Materazzi's position. After all, if the law cannot act against the *voyou,* why should that same *voyou* not proclaim itself "innocent" through situating itself apolitically? Within the "normal" scheme of rhetorical things, Materazzi is probably right, but what the event reveals is how simultaneously routine and radical the event is. It requires only a small break with the normative, a small rent in the discursive fabric, to produce a critical rupture with the usual order of things. All that was required to produce this event was, it turns out, the secret. The event is rooted in the routine, "visible," and secret, thinkable but unknowable in advance of itself. The event is its own time; the event is the thinking of history in the now without understanding, as will be discussed later, the complexity of the relationship between the apolitical and sovereignty.

In this regard, what happened "between" Zidane and Materazzi (as if such an encounter can be artificially foreclosed, making any form of limited engagement—"between"—a putative description) reveals how the event cannot be rendered as a matter of individual capacity, or incapacity. In these terms, Zidane's transgression stems from his "inability" to allow for the discursively permissible—under the rubric of which Materazzi would include "son of a terrorist whore" or some derivation thereof. The event cannot be explained as the accountability or liability of a single player (or two single players acting in concert to bring about the event), even though Zidane's signality is, literally, constitutive of the event. The event could not be more appropriately named, *coup de boule,* because it is made up of his head (Zidane), made in their heads (Zidane and Materazzi), made by their heads, in the moment, some would have it, that Zidane "lost his head" and replaced thought with, paradoxically, the use of cranial force. (The phrase "losing one's head" describes that moment when, as colloquially insinuated, the *voyou* does not think but acts without forethought, without thought for the consequences of his unthought act; when one, momentarily at least, gives up one's head; when "emotions" overwhelm reason. In this instance, paradoxically, this phrase is wholly wrong, because how does the *voyou* act with his head unless he has thought about using his head? Does not all action begin with thought? How could it not? After all, where does, where can, the event—the action of head butting, of pitting cranium against sternum, pitting head ["the unthinking" moment] against head [the thought that provoked the *coup de boule*]—begin but in the head of the *voyou*?) The *coup de boule* is the event that exists now, in its most potent political form (that is to say, it endures, it lives, it has since the event lived), in all our heads. Zidane's head symbolically transferred itself through its forcefulness against Materazzi into our political imaginaries. The event was headed, with the kind of unerring power, accuracy, and sure placement of a Zidane header, straight from the TV screen (straight from Berlin) into our store of cultural knowledge, unsettling us, disturbing our heads—disturbing us in our heads. Zidane did nothing, in effecting the event (that memorable flick of his formidable forehead), but think himself into our heads so that we might, must, now think him, think with him—think him as the thought of the *voyou,* as how sinuously, how insistent and insidiously, the thought of the *voyou* moves. (Or how, Jacobus might suggest, the "singularity" of Zidane–Materazzi as the *voyou* confronts us with the challenge of thinking the *voyou* always as nothing less than "juxtaposition, divergence, and difference"—or arguably, as "juxtaposition, divergence, and difference" first and foremost.) The event has become nothing less than the thought of Zidane, disjunctively, synthetically linked, of course, to the provocation and the instigation that tests the limits of discursive possibility—that is, Materazzi's thought. The force of the cranial act is such that it leaves nothing unthought. Paradigmatically phrased, such is the cranial force of the act of thought: the force of thinking the event begins in, and with, the head. Most importantly, the event exists only as thought for all, as it is thought by all, because it is thought by all, beginning, in this instance, with Zidane and Materazzi. The *coup de boule* as the event demands, first, that it be understood as the effect of thinking. The event is the thought of the athletic body in motion, the body as thought moves in it, the movement of (hyperkinetic) thought. The event is the effect of the political, the political distilled to thought itself, the political as nothing other than the time of thought.

In this way, the time of the event belongs properly to the time of history. This is precisely the case with *l'affaire Zizou*. The event of Zidane constitutes a form of subtractive practice because it could not be contained by the time of its own making (sport, the cultural spectacle), the time of Berlin (the truncated, specific time of the World Cup final; first 90 minutes, then 120 minutes), or the (extended, historic) time of the banlieue to which Zizou, Frenchman of Kabyle ancestry, traced his immediate origins. The event of Zidane can only be thought as the multiple time of history, in no small measure because it changed—in the moment of the *coup de boule*—the history of the Coupe du Monde. The event of Zidane must thought in this way because, and this is the secret lodged at the heart of the secret, it subtracts—under the force of the philosophical interrogative—so insistently (and, occasionally, even artfully) into question the law's inability to account for the *voyou*. Zizou may have been subtracted from the field of play when he was sent off (indicated by the red card the referee showed him), but his dismissal is precisely what broke the bonds of football (sports) discourse. His subtraction let loose the multiple, released History into play; the event is known, then, by its capacity to generate the multiple, to open us up to the multiple through refusing the singular suture, that rendering of the Situation that seeks to restrict it to a singular explication.

THE SECRET

The secret is always the shared act, the intimate exchange, the secret that is only partially, and, therefore, more powerfully, a secret. The secret is always shared because the secret always exists, circulates, outside the self, outside the secret itself; the secret is never secret. The secret is not silence; the secret is loud reverberation, as the event of the *voyou* Zizou and Materazzi makes clear. Nothing speaks louder than the secret because the secret may concern (contain) the hidden (or private) matters that are publicly unspeakable, and, therefore, eminently audible in other registers—registers, that is, that resonate (count) publicly even when the unspeakable is not spoken.

In the moment of the *coup de boule* or, perhaps more accurately, in the moment just before the head was used, in the moment that the head decided "enough," the secret ceased to be a secret. After all, how could it continue to be a secret when the whole world was invited, literally, to watch the event? The secret that was no longer a secret irrupted the time of the game, and as such, it became the time of the event, became the event itself; as the secret that was no longer secret, it remained (un)locked on a patch of green grass in a Berlin stadium, a stadium in a city that was itself once famously divided and full of secrets, a city that lived between two times, a time filled with history and secrets, a history of a city prefixed "East" and "West," a history of secrets that flooded through a wall, in 1989, and continues today to make itself public in the blatant inequality between the historic East and West, a city in which two sets of secrets lived in all-too-proximate danger of each other—secrets that lived separately, secrets that collided, secrets that depended on each other's existence for their own livelihood, secrets that inveighed against and invaded each other, sometimes in the same moment, occasionally in and through the same gesture. Berlin: there could not be a more appropriate city in which the secret could take up dwelling—where the secret could live as itself, by itself, and far beyond itself.

The secret is necessarily more than itself because it exceeds the time and space in which it was conceived. The secret is, in this instance, the *voyou*—roguish, irascible, mobile—so that it can live in public. Whether or not the secret is fully known, it can never live (only) in private, despite, of course, the paradoxical recognition that the secret cannot, in any effect, ever be fully known. To extend the contradiction, the secret lives its privacy in public, so that it is never either fully public or private.

The event of the *coup de boule* became an event only when the world was "invited" into the already passed, but now impossible-to-pass, time of Zidane and Materazzi. In the moment of the turning to the past, when the event began to live outside itself, the secret could no longer be a secret, even as the details of the physical exchange (the head butt apart, that is) and the rhetorical particulars of the exchange remained hidden. In its multitudinous aftermath, in its becoming an event, it opened itself up to the secret's greatest threat and single greatest advantage: speculation about the content of the secret. What did Materazzi say? Are we to trust what Materazzi said? Why would we trust Materazzi? Why not? Had Materazzi said anything to Zidane before?

All secrets, by their imagining of themselves as precluding knowledge, their priding themselves on their inexplicability and their power of foreclosure, their capacity to retain information to themselves (rhetorical and political prophylaxis), both promise their survival and threaten themselves. The secret can only live with, and as, the threat of revelation—that it will become known. That is the power of the secret. That is also its most profound vulnerability: what it imagines is not known may already be partially known, or speculated about, or in existence as rumor or fact; it may already belong to the public's store of shared knowledge; there may be no power in what it reveals. The secret has to live moment to moment with the threat of exposure. Materazzi may even finally be outed—he may tell us exactly what it is he said (or exactly what it is he recalls he said; how different will it be from the speculations that will have, by then, existed for years?). But how much will it matter then, if at all?

The inefficacy of the "confession" was already evident in September 2006, just barely a month after the event, when Materazzi offered his account of the secret. He claimed it, in the spirit of the apolitical, as an insult to Zidane's sister. Given its temporal proximity to the event, it left no mark on the event because it failed to ameliorate—because it could not stand as a truth—the politics of the event. Materazzi's confession had no effect on the event because nothing in what he said afterward—the afterword that is not, can never be, the final word; it is simply another concatenated word—offered itself as a thinking of the event itself.[8] Without thinking the event, no word, certainly no confession, no afterword, can have any standing in relation to the secret—to the event. That is to say, the confession is a priori an insufficient mode of reasoning with the event.

However, what Materazzi's afterword makes clear is the threat of the secret. The effect of the secret is such that the secret, the unspeakable that registers as spoken, becomes absolute danger, absolute threat. The secret is nothing other than the private revealing its full public face, its full face in public. The secret is the private declaring itself as what it always is: a document of public record, a document always phrased in a language that is known. The threat of the secret is that it can never be contained to, within itself; the secret, perforce, exceeds itself, makes itself other to itself—the secret is always more than itself and, consequently, less than itself. The secret is less than itself because it does not matter what Materazzi said to Zidane. It matters only that he said it—that he said it repeatedly, according to Zidane—and that the event is borne out of Zidane's limit: the event is that Zidane found Materazzi's pronouncement(s) unacceptable. Zidane would not let Materazzi say what he did anymore. Zidane would not allow Materazzi's enunciation, those (offensive, to be sure) phrases uttered in the heat of the action, those under-the-breath mutterings, insults, that trash talk, that mano a mano bantering, to go unanswered. The event of the *coup de boule* is the *voyou* speaking to the *voyou,* through the head, to the body—and the head—of the (offending, lower level, incendiary) *voyou.* In this regard, the event of the *voyou* speaks directly to the matter of law's inability to address—let alone legislate—behavior. The *voyou* shows how uncertain the law is about its reach into behavior because the *voyou*'s actions may concern behavior that is privately considered objectionable—Materazzi labeling Zidane's mother a "terrorist whore" or his sister a "prostitute"—but is publicly judged legal (or only illegal in a "minor" way). The secret and the *voyou* not only both raise the issue of private–public demarcation but also raise it in its relation to pronouncement. The secret can be known, but not publicly pronounced; the behavior of the *voyou* can be condemned—it is impermissible, not allowed, to denounce someone's mother as a "terrorist whore" in private—but not publicly pronounced as culpable. Culpable of what? A transgressive speech act? Hate speech? On a football field, as we know, all manner of discursive transgressions occur—racist speech, homophobic speech, speech filled with sectarian invective, speech dripping with vile nationalism, sometimes friendly banter between opponents, and speech aimed by players at opponents, by spectators ranting at and taunting players, and—a much less frequent practice—by players responding in kind to fans. In this way, the event of Zidane raises culpability to an entirely new political level. (This incarnation of the *voyou,* as footballer—as footballer taunting footballer—demonstrates how the idiomatic particularity of the realm opens up a very specific set of questions; yet of course, it also shows how the law, in any formulation, provokes questions about itself, questions that obtain on and off the football field.) And, because the secret is something illicit, the *voyou* must be the illicit subject that can be, is, recognized as such but cannot be publicly, or officially, at least, condemned as such. Football may recognize the tendencies of the *voyou,* but it is as yet unable to name him—or her—as such.

In this way, what Zidane and Materazzi make public is how the *voyou* reveals the limits of the law's reach and, importantly, inverts the private–public demarcation. (There is, however, an innate tension between Zidane and Materazzi as *voyous.* This articulation depends on a coming-together—at first surprising, then explicable—between Zidane and Materazzi that then diverges into a conflict about the integrity of the *voyou.* What kind of *voyou* seeks to expose his fellow to the law? Or is that the ultimate *voyou* trick?) In the event, it is Materazzi who is the "first" *voyou*. In speaking to Zidane, he literally taunts the law because he knows that the law cannot legislate his behavior; he knows that it cannot tell him what he might (not) say in private. "Liberated" by the law that has no jurisdiction over him, Materazzi is free, as it were, to pronounce Zizou's sister a *puttana,* his mother a "terrorist whore." In public, Materazzi will only say that what he did was nothing "unusual"; he preserves the secret by reserving to himself the right to speak the secret only in terms that are permissible—"unusual," a term intended to cover, as it were, a multitude of impermissibles. At the same time, of course, he is bringing the secret into public by casting it as not being unusual; in this articulation, he provokes questions about the secret (What, exactly, was said? Why can it not be repeated? If what was said was not "unusual," why can it not be made public?). Because of his provocation (or titillation), Materazzi denudes the secret of any private aspect (any right to privacy) and, in so doing, not only makes the secret a public matter but also threatens the secret as secret. Contained in any provocation is the threat to make the secret known. Materazzi the *voyou* inaugurates the *voyou* as the keeper of the secret and, in this way, reconceives, to his detriment, the role of the illicit subject by drawing himself into that role. Materazzi's act not only makes him the guardian of illicit information but also removes the aura—in a vernacularly Benjaminian sense—and (possibly) the prophylaxis that the designation *voyou* offers. Because of how Materazzi exploits the *voyou*'s position, he may no longer be entitled to the protection inherent in that role. In this instance, the *voyou* may have proven too clever for his own good. By overplaying his hand rhetorically, the *voyou* risks forfeiting the insulation against indictment that inheres in the roguishness of the *voyou*. Materazzi reveals the opacity of the *voyou*: he makes the *voyou* and its mode of action visible; we can "see" what the *voyou* does, how he does it (how he disables the law), and, as importantly, why. In so doing, Materazzi makes the *voyou* vulnerable.

As a *voyou* who keeps the secret, Materazzi reveals himself as the speaker of what is considered both privately and publicly objectionable. Materazzi says in private what he will not say in public; he says in private what he knows is impermissible in public and, in so doing, gives public life to the secret. Because of his fidelity to the secret, Materazzi assigns himself, unwittingly, the role of *le voyou*—he is the petty criminal who seeks the protection, the immunization, of the secret; his reliance on (putative) normality shows him to be not so much ordinary as disputatious and disingenuous. He uses the notion of normality—not having done anything "unusual"—to deny what he did; Materazzi wants to use the secret to protect himself while simultaneously claiming that he has nothing to hide—he has behaved in a manner "usual" for a footballer—and that he has no use for the secret. All the while, of course, Materazzi behaves as if we were all in on the (public) secret—behaves as if he were saying what he does with a wink and, in the process, is trying to hoodwink us.

The secret protects only itself; it harbors no loyalty to those who are bound to and by it. Such people are threatened by the secret precisely because they are so bound to it; they are made vulnerable by their implication in it, their reliance on it. The secret is incapable of a broader loyalty. *Le voyou* is, of course, not a role Materazzi wants, but sometimes, as in this instance, the *voyou* catches himself in it because of the intricate rhetorical web he has spun. In outwitting the law by exploiting its limitation, it is in his (unreciprocated) felicity to the terms of the secret that the *voyou* (à la Materazzi) indicts himself. Materazzi shows himself to be, as are all athletes who engage in private trash talking, a "petty criminal" of a not very high order. He is the *voyou* who relies on the sanctity, if we might call it that (we might also name it a reliance on the "privacy" of the secret), of the private. Materazzi says in private that for which he would be condemned, and possibly indicted (if it transgresses the law), in public. In relying so heavily on the terms (the sanctity) of the secret, Materazzi shows nothing so much as his imperfect comprehension of, to phrase it awkwardly, the self-interested political of the secret. In attaching himself so closely to the secret, the discourse of unexceptionality—his transgression merits no special opprobrium; he did nothing "unusual"—and his hope for a lack of public sanction (because of the limits of the law) to insulate him, Materazzi makes himself vulnerable to his counterpart (that part that belongs also, in part, to him), the *voyou* whose act reveals the limits of the law's reach. Materazzi is the *voyou* whose actions bring the opacity of the *voyou* to life. Because of what he did, Materazzi activates the *voyou* (Zidane) against the *voyou* (Materazzi)—the *voyou* who has been acted against (Zidane) by a fellow *voyou* is free to do as he pleases. Shouldn't this be the *voyou* code of honor?

Because of how Materazzi repurposes the role of *voyou,* he creates the conditions that allow for the usurpation—possibly even the insolvency—of his instantiation of the *voyou*. In effect, because of what Materazzi does, Zidane has to do little but remain silent—he must remain disciplined in his nonspeaking—to restore the integrity of the *voyou* to itself. Because it is presumed, with some veracity, that Materazzi said in private what is publicly impermissible, it is in and through Zidane's silence that he reveals the law's inability to regulate behavior. Zizou did what he did because the law could not prevent Materazzi from saying what he said with impunity, with no risk of retribution. In saying nothing after his act (Situation), after the event (the Situation that gathered multiple Situations into itself to make the event), his silence, unlike Materazzi's failed recourse to the secret, Zidane—silently, letting the resonant image of his head, as it were, do the talking—continued to do nothing less than what the *voyou* properly should: raise questions about the reach of the law; draw the law into question. Why did the law allow Materazzi to speak as he did in an encounter that may have been private in nature but took place in an entirely public venue, in a spectacle, the World Cup, that could not have been more public?

At its core, then, the secret is both contradictory and confusing. It is presumed to be private, but it is intensely public. Its first

commitment is to prophylaxis of the self, yet it invites speculation. The secret is as capable of acting for itself as it is of being
coopted by others—for purposes that are often self-interested,
even nefarious. The secret is confusing in that it lends itself easily
to prevarication, obfuscation, or, as in Materazzi's case, denial;
the secret can, in short, make it difficult to establish with any
certainty what is going on, what has gone on. In regard to Zidane
and Materazzi, the secret refers to what Materazzi said to Zidane
(what could not be heard and might never be known) and to the
history and politics that constitute the meaning of the event but
could not be spoken. The secret, then, has a complex structure
(composed, like the event, of a series of Situations) in that what
is perceived as the content of the structure—what is said, what
was done—is invariably merely a part of its formal structure. The
actual content of the secret is hidden—publicly obscured—not
so much by silence (although the decision not to speak is a critical one; sometimes it constitutes the very ground of the secret)
as by substitution, as by, in Materazzi's case, the substitution of
"unusual" for the precise words that were exchanged. (Can those
words ever be correctly recalled? Surely that utterance can never
be recovered.)

The secret is generative because the act of substitution opens,
as happened in the event, the possibility for speculation. This is
how words that may or may not have been part of the speech act
itself—pejorative terms, derogations—not only come to take the
place of what was or may have been said but supplement, aug-
ment, embellish, or even subtract from the substitution. In other
words, substitution is itself not only a mark of conceptual inadequacy but the invitation to overwrite—to write out, itself a kind
of subtractive practice—the substitution itself. The substitution
is always in danger of being overwhelmed by its own (perceived)
inadequacy. After all, the very fact of substitution provokes nothing so much as the desire to substitute the substitution for the
speech act itself. The violence done to the substitution expresses,
not to put too fine a point on it, the desire for the true language

of the secret. The violence done to the substitution is a felicitous act in that it seeks to return the secret to itself and, in so doing, restore truth to the event.

Yet the preoccupation with the secret of what Materazzi actually said to Zidane itself functions as a substitution. In fact, this might be the true structure of the secret: the preoccupation with what is actually said serves only to not address the history of what is said. Attending to what was said is a means of not addressing the secret history (the secret of history) that spoke through Materazzi's words, no matter what he said. It is not simply, then, that Materazzi resorted, we might speculate, to misogynistic terms *(puttana)* or to racist, xenophobic ones—which he denies having said (terms that might have been blatantly anti-Islamic, redolent as the term is with post-9/11 anti-Islamic bias, all of which might be contained in the phrase "son of a terrorist whore")—but that the laws of football have no way of outlawing such language, of outlawing such behavior. It is this, the game's history and politics, that is still secret (even as it is widely known), that needs to be elucidated; it is the game's history of not attending to the kind of language Materazzi deems "usual," of treating that behavior as if it were inherently part of the game, of tolerating this behavior (and, if the game has for decades done nothing in terms of trying to stamp out racism, xenophobia, and so on, then its having done nothing amounts to something approximating condoning it),[9] that constitutes the secret at the core of the substitution that is itself constitutive of the secret.

Through his actions as *voyou,* which stand in contradistinction to Materazzi's *voyou* behavior, Zidane tries to restore integrity to the *voyou*—even as he raises the question as to whether such a restoration is possible, whether it is not only the law that must be interrogated but how the *voyou* itself is thought. After all, are we to trust Zidane's classic nonapology apology, what Alice Kaplan has named a "classic *je m'en excuse, mais je ne regrette pas*" ("I apologize, but I do not regret it")?[10] Isn't that, the classic nonapology apology, the rhetorical strategist's greatest skill?

Zidane's national TV "apology" was truly an unforgettable public performance. Clad in a high-end fashion "military fatigue-style" jacket, he spoke slowly, pronouncing deliberately almost every syllable of every word, and gently, repeatedly invoking children, pronouncing himself sorry that his actions might have been inappropriate for them; and teachers, too, got their fair share of attention (because they instruct the young and impressionable in morality, in the difference between right and wrong). In that apology, Zizou created a bizarre disjuncture between his faux battle garb and his, a Canal+ TV commentator suggested, "childlike" manner. Did he especially address children because children alone might have been improperly influenced by the nature, scope, and intensity of the event? Did this make children alone deserving of an apology? Or, as is more likely the case, is it that Zidane did not want to set a "bad example" (as *Le Monde* lamented in its July 10, 2006, edition), having, of course, done precisely that and then compounded the error by explaining his actions sans apology?

In the TV interview, the (banlieue) warrior had, it seemed, become a crafty, *voyou*-like "Bambi." However, the measured quality of his speech recalled the deliberateness of his actions during the event. In both instances, there is the visage of Zidane's head ominously poised and headed for the chest of another. First it was Materazzi's chest in Berlin, and then the image returned a few days later in Paris during Zidane's tête-à-tête with French president Jacques Chirac. Shaking hands with the French leader, in his fatigue jacket, Zizou stands at just such an angle to the camera that his head is inclined toward Chirac, as if to repeat the event by head butting the head of state—not only transgressing against the law of the game but acting, with forethought, with thoughtful intent, against the sovereign. It did not happen, of course, but it was so spectrally evocative in the Zizou–Chirac encounter as to suggest not only the mobility of the event but how—even in what might be imagined as the most unusual of locales—the event is never out of place: first in

Berlin, then in Paris, from one European capital to another, all over Europe, it seems: first on the most hallowed of sport's occasions, the final of the World Cup, and then in what we might name the confessional—the conversation between subject and sovereign, called at the sovereign's behest. The history of the event makes, as it were, every moment, every occasion, a time in which the event can occur again, as if for the first time, as if the event belongs, properly, everywhere, all the time.

What was politically salient about the Zizou–Chirac meeting was that the French president "forgave" Zidane in public: hence, the spectacle of ruler and ruled, Frenchman to Frenchman, addressing each other. Chirac forgave Zidane like a Catholic priest granting absolution, only this time in the name of the sovereign, not God. In this encounter, Chirac acts as the Schmittian sovereign. The sovereign, says Schmitt, is "he who determines the exception." Following this logic, it is possible to argue that the event constitutes the exceptional moment and, as such, is tantamount to a declaration of sovereignty: the event is the event because it stands alone, by itself, exceptional. In this regard, the event lends the *voyou* a form of singularity, though not of course sovereignty itself, but something sufficiently proximate that the sovereign must respond, is compelled by the event to respond. Zidane is not, of course, declaring an abrogation of the laws for the state of emergency, but Chirac recognizes that something of historic significance is happening, something that requires him to act publicly, in the wake of the event, and symbolically "reinstate" himself as sovereign. (Chirac meeting Zidane in public amounts to the state ordaining the event as event.) On one hand, the sovereignty of Chirac remains firmly in place; on the other, his calling Zidane to him—interpellation, an old-fashioned hailing, making the subject of the state a subject again, in public— suggests that Chirac understands that he again needs to coopt the *voyou*. (The sovereign cannot leave the *voyou*'s actions to go unremarked on, but neither can it publicly rebuke, reprimand, or punish the rogue because the *voyou* commands, through his actions and his silence, a constituency; the *voyou* belongs to that part that constitutes an implicit challenge, if not outright threat, to the sovereign.) In the act of public address (the confessional, interpellation), the *voyou* can be shown to be addressed but not brought under control; the *voyou*'s behavior can be acknowledged but not regulated after the event (it is, in any case, already too late); the *voyou,* most importantly, can be brought to heel gently, through a diplomatic engagement in the most sacrosanct halls of power. The Kabyle can be made part of the state again, quickly, without being castigated. Chirac's act speaks of an attempt to restore the *voyou* to the status of subject. The *voyou* cannot, must not, be allowed to retain its status any longer than is absolutely necessary. That is the work the event assigns the sovereign—or the warning the event issues the sovereign.

The sovereign, especially, knows its vulnerability to the *voyou,* and so, in place of condemnation, there is in the Zidane–Chirac encounter something akin to the *voyou* "confessing" and the sovereign "absolving." And so there is in the exchange between the sovereign and the *voyou* a secret, one that mitigates, works actively (as we have come to expect), against history and politics. The confessional is, of course, a private exchange, so that even when it is performed in public between the president and the footballer, it remains secret. No one other than Chirac and Zidane is privy to their exchange, except as a spectacle (or, the spectacle, designed for public consumption, that follows the confessional). The spectacle may be a matter of no small public import, but the sovereignty of the exchange, protected as it is by the state, is never under threat of disclosure. Here, again, the secret, but this time in an un-*voyou*-like fashion, retains its integrity by submitting to the laws—or the decorum, if you wish—of the state. The secret is publicly foreclosed, except in that historic visage—Zidane inclining toward Chirac. It is only the threat that comes from outside the state, from outside the sovereign, that cannot be foreclosed. More specifically, Zidane is the threat that emanates, in two senses (his Kabyle origins; the event in Berlin), from outside France itself.

In this instance, the secret can (again) pretend that one obscurity—the secret that produced the event in Berlin—can be undone by another; by pretending that the secret of and to the event with the sovereign in Paris is, or, at least, could have been, unlocked—rendered sovereignly public, to coin an awkward phrase—in the inner sanctum of sovereign power after which it is reenacted, full of phantasms, on the steps of the presidential palace. In this encounter lies the real danger of the secret. When Zidane and Chirac meet, whether face-to-face or, phantasmagorically, head-to-chest, the secret comes into its own by pretending—performing—its own, voluntary, liquidation; the secret exposes itself for all to see. When Zidane and Chirac stand before the crowd, the secret pretends a certain kind of unlocking—an unlocking that turns on the optical, not the aural; on the image, not the word. When Zidane and Chirac stand together before the crowd, they offer a public display of confession, forgiveness, and penitence. What has been witnessed, putatively, presumptively, formally, is the public spilling of the secret. That the secret is no more is clear, there for all to see. However, all that is witnessed is the secret, once again, immunizing itself against disclosure—the actual historical matter of the secret, the secret itself, has again been hidden away. This time, even more so than in Berlin (where the secret acquired life only after the fact), the secret is hidden in full public view.

Therein, paradoxically, resides both the secret's autoimmunity and its obscurity, for want of a better term. It may be that the event is the secret, open, everywhere, visible, but somehow still obscure. Necessarily so, because the event is rendered in an idiom that is unique to the event out of which it arises—the field, the stadium, the political situation. Of course, a trace of it is rendered publicly. We see this most often when, say, an athlete breaks a record and the event reverberates across various media, from the field to the stands to TV and the Internet, and in our times, it proliferates with lightning speed across the social networking media. The sporting event reverberates in part because of its scarcity (a twenty-five-year-old record is not broken every day) but more so because of its ubiquity: it happens, and the eventfulness—what some might term its media-worthiness—is determined by the intensity of the event. That is the only measure, in sport, of the event: how, and for how long, we must add, does it reverberate? How long does the event stay with us? How long does it present itself to us across the media spectrum? Most important, does the event make us think? Is intensity the provocation to thinking? Intensity, in this rendering, functions as *différance* does for Derrida. *Différance* (which the sports event shows us is not just for high modern literature) is everywhere, maybe even much more intensely in sport than in, say, Mallarmé.

THE VOYOU'S SINGULARITY

All the while, of course, the sovereign understands Zidane's singularity. Zizou is not so much the *voyou* as such—the pure, if you will, *voyou*—but the privileged *voyou,* the *voyou* with a différance. After France's victory, on home soil, in the 1998 Coupe du Monde, the Marseilles-born Zidane became the most visible and successful product, the cultural face, of Republican France's triumph (the subsumption of difference into, in the cause of, national triumph); Zizou was, like some of his colleagues (Lilian Thuram most prominent among them), the face of the banlieue's integration into the French Republic—the success of French indifference to difference, a triumph over Le Pen's xenophobia. In the aftermath of that 1998 victory, Zizou became—literally—not only the poster boy for the success of French Republicanism, not only the "face" of the multiracial nation, but its public "head." After that 1998 World Cup win over Brazil (Zizou scored twice), it seemed that his head looked down on the French nation from every billboard.

On the grounds of his historic exceptionality, the Kabyle Zidane was, we presume, eight years later granted clemency by the sovereign. Conversely, those other Berbers (the native inhabitants of the Maghreb, those whose presence in North Africa predates the Arab conquest), Beurs (French-born, second-generation Al-gerians who, like Zizou, came of age in France; Beurs are French citizens), and Arabs ("anyone of Maghrebi appearance is liable to be referred to by a French observer as an Arab"[11]) from those self-same suburban ghettoes in Paris and Marseille, among other places, who had taken to the streets to act against the brutality of the police in October 2005, would never be candidates for sovereign grace.

The place of the Beur, metonymically speaking, in the French nation was at the penal core that is France's suburban periphery, the banlieue—not, publicly, like Zidane, disclosing the secret, keeping the company of the absolution-granting sovereign. The Beur who is not Zidane is excluded through what amounts to carceral inclusion, that is, restricted to the occluded life of the banlieue. Unlike Zidane, those other banlieue heads could be sacrificed to the law of the state—in part, of course, because it could never lead, had never led, would never lead (or head, since Zizou stood at the head of the nation's football accomplishments) the nation to glory. Or, depending on your point of view, head the republic to eventful infamy in 2006, infamy that threatened to erase the glory that Zidane and his black colleagues (Thuram, again, prominent among them) brought to the republic in 1998, and again in 2000, when it won the European championships. In 2000, it was a triumph over Italy, of course, as historical irony would have it. Zidane, then, both can (or is made to) and cannot stand for all the other residents of the banlieue—on one hand, he is exceptional (and singular); on the other, he is rendered "unfit" for any form of representation because of the *coup de boule*. Or the very physicality and violence of his act returns him, in Le Pen's discourse, to the only place for which he is fit. The hero of 1998 instantiates the triumph of the republic; the villain (or *voyou*) of 2006 reveals the ineradicability of the banlieue.

In this discordant rendering of Zidane, there exists a dis-junctive synthesis—the "different" "Zidanes" must be thought together—because there is no difference in intensity. All that must be thought here is the uniqueness of the idiom, that is, the first turn of the event. For Zizou and Materazzi, this means, first, the interaction that emerges out of language (the language of the game, the language of the secret), the law, and *voyou*. The idiom, this particular idiom, returns us to the event out of which it arises. (And, in the case of Zidane, as we shall see, ubiquity is always a matter that demands consideration.) Contained within the idiom, as Geoffrey Bennington delineates it in "DerridaBase" (his "conversation" with Derrida), is *différance*: "the delay or lateness that means that meaning is always anticipated or established after the event."[12]

Zizou makes publicly visible the public secret of what is publicly known: not all *voyous* or banlieue residents are equal; the exceptional athlete is more equal than (almost) any other; Zidane has an exceptional political status, a status that enables him to create and be privy to a secret to which even the sovereign wants to be privy, even if only symbolically—if only to demonstrate publicly the force of sovereignty. Because of his exceptionality, Zidane draws into question the relation between the *voyou* and the great athlete. What, exactly, is the relation? Are they one thing, the *voyou* and the exceptional athlete, or two?

The answer to these questions is, in fact, surprisingly simple—reductive, even. The star athlete can be a *voyou* at least as long as the *voyou* is a star athlete or a star athlete who continues to resonate publicly (or the star athlete who has just retired under the most historic of conditions: the event). In the terms of this argument, the star athlete relates to the *voyou* in the most peculiar way: the star athlete is neither one thing (star athlete) nor two (star athlete and *voyou*) but a presentation of things that can be, for the glory of the nation, folded into one, depending on the moment (Zidane as French national hero in 1998 and 2000, Beur, or worse, in 2006); the two can be rendered indistinguishable so that each is neither one thing nor the other; the star athlete Zidane is capable of being one thing (star athlete) that ameliorates (for Chirac) or exacerbates (for Le Pen) the other *(voyou)*. What the event reveals, in this regard, is the public secret of the star athlete. The star athlete is, finally, known not by his (or her) exceptionality but by the utter contingency of his stardom, or, in Zidane's case, by the ways in which the star athlete is always haunted by the shadow of the *voyou*. The public secret of the event is that the event can make the star athlete, without hesitation, nothing but the *voyou*—the *voyou* who must be absolved by Chirac and is condemned by Le Pen.

The event of Zidane makes evident the full complexity of the interplay among the event, the *voyou,* and the secret. The strange thing about the "secret event" of Zidane is that it took place, was played out, if you will, entirely in public. In fact, it was extensively discussed, dissected, and examined for deeper meaning—it was an intensely public event. However, what makes it an event of a peculiarly secret nature is the particular quality of the *voyou*. The event of Zidane shows that the *voyou,* unlike the criminal but like (as) the athlete, can perform in public; his behavior can even set in motion a world of discourse, some of which is admiring; what he does can, in fact, be seen as something of a deft achievement, a political achievement, even—the indefatigability of the banlieue, the irrepressibility of the banlieue, the banlieue's capacity to haunt the republic, not only within its own borders but in another European city, before the very eyes of the football-watching world. In this way, what the event of Zidane "leaves us is," as Derrida says of the legacy of Paul de Man, "the gift of an ordeal."[13] The "gift" of the "ordeal," the challenge (and, indeed, the invitation) of thinking the difficulty of the Zidane event, is that there will always be something indefinite and unstateable—silence, the secret—about what the *voyou* does because the *voyou* acts on the border of the law so that it is almost impossible to say what the law can do in relation to the *voyou*—and so that it is almost impossible to say what the *voyou* does to the law, except that we know it does something. At the very least, we know there is nothing to do but face the "ordeal": stand up to it, or, in Chirac's case, stand next to it and make the sovereign vulnerable to it (as Derrida's speaking for de Man made him vulnerable), and think the demands it makes on the thought of the event, the secret, and our understanding of the *voyou*.

THE ORDEAL FOR SOVEREIGNTY

The purpose, in this chapter, of thinking the category "sport" and the category "*voyou*" together has been to put into question, in two ways, the reach of the law. This thinking of Zidane and Materazzi reveals a salient, we might even say surprising, relationship between the sporting figure and the sovereign. It is not simply a matter of resemblance but of hauntology—thinking Zidane in relationship makes evident the ways in which the sporting figure troubles the sovereign. We come, through this process, to understand the particular signality of sport—especially of the sporting figure. The sporting figure may be, like the sovereign, above the law (but still within the rules of the game; the sovereign, of course, has no such strictures because the sovereign can make up the rules—that is, maintain, change, or ignore them). At the same time, the *voyou* may be beneath these rules—not worthy of the law's consideration, condemned to living beneath the law, to living, that is, in the banlieue, susceptible only to the repressive force of the law. However, it is when the star athlete is from the banlieue (even if he is no longer of it; yet he is always presumed to be, especially in the event, of it) that his relation to the banlieue becomes most difficult to articulate, most vexing, that it provokes the greatest number of questions, raises the greatest anxiety, about itself, about the law, about sovereignty. So much so that, as we see with Chirac, the sovereign must address the *voyou* in public so that the entire republic can see, even (or especially?) those French *citoyens* who hail from the banlieue, the place—there is a place, albeit a surveilled place—for the *voyou*; the body of the star athlete can be displayed to the republic, even when the *voyou* has brought the event into being.

It may be, tautologically phrased, precisely the issue of sovereignty that marks the sporting figure, that explains why sport always presents itself as a political difficulty for sovereignty. It is the event of sovereignty, variously articulated though it is, staged in a range of venues and each with its own local and international evocations, that is shared by Artest, Cantona, and Zidane: the sporting figure will always be a figure of sovereignty. Sovereignty knows this, whether or not sovereignty knows this. The sporting figure has access to sovereignty's deepest secret. The sporting figure provides, like the *voyou,* visible proof that something about the law is uncertain in its comprehension. The sporting figure makes visible that there is something the sovereign knows about itself, which is this: that it does not, cannot, can never, fully know itself; that there is a force of sovereignty not beyond but within sovereignty itself, a force that emerges in the most unlikely, un-expected moment, in full view of the public—that is to say, right before the sovereign. What could sovereignty and the law want made visible, made publicly, spectacularly visible, less than that?

And this provokes the secret contradiction about the politics of sport, or sport and politics—or the secret that the politics of sport resides in its being simultaneously, in regard to sovereignty, a political and an apolitical practice. On one hand, sport is always political not so much because it manifests history and politics both publicly and secretly as because it always displays the potential—and perhaps displacing and compromising the potential—of the state of exception, the sacred, constitutive province of the sover-eign. On the other, sport may be apolitical not because it is outside racial, national, class, or gender politics (it rarely is) but because it calls into visibility what is beyond the reach of sovereignty. Or through the event (such is the force of the event), the star athlete can become the figure of sovereignty that is not the sovereign, that figure whose sovereignty is not delineable, does not give itself up for statement easily, if at all. And yet, of course, it is a figure that is, in the event, capable of speaking through the event.

That is the secret of the sports figure and the *voyou,* the sports figure as *voyou.* The sports figure is the secret of sovereignty that is not the sovereign, the secret sovereignty that is always, it would appear, alternately, first one and then the other, at rest and in motion, fully visible to sovereignty, fully within sovereignty. Yet the sovereignty of the sports figure is such that it is always beyond the reach of sovereign law. This is what sovereignty confronts in Artest (on the scorer's table) and Cantona (by force of law, banned from the game) at rest and glimpses in the motion of Artest and Cantona (in their going into the stands). This is what sovereignty recognizes in Zidane in that moment with Chirac: the inextricable coexistence of sovereignty in the athlete in motion and at rest. In that public encounter with Chirac, Zidane pro-poses (suggests; stands cinematically as) an unrestful, restive, at-restness, as he stands, cinematically, perhaps literally, poised for violence against the sovereign. For (Chirac's) sovereignty (or any sovereign/ty), nothing could be more shocking, more disabling, more arresting, than coming face-to-face with sovereignty over which it is not sovereign: the secret face of sovereignty that is not secret. Perhaps that is, on second thought, more arresting to sovereignty—the fact that the secret is visible and, as a consequence, is not secret after all. The gift of the event of the sports figure is truly an un-welcome ordeal for sovereignty.

A secret is necessarily a violent thing in that its retention requires that a violence be done, almost daily, to the self; it de-mands, in its ipseity (its selfness), that violence be done to those with whom the self comes into contact. There will always be, from now on, on Zizou, the trace of Coupe du Monde violence, a singular violence that makes nothing (and, of course, everything to his critics) of his previous outbursts of anger on the field, his previous head butt. In the 2000–1 season, while playing—as historical irony would have it—for the Italian giants, Juventus, in the European Champions League competition against the German side, SV Hamburg, Zidane head butted Jochen Kientz. It was one of Zidane's fourteen career red cards. The most ignominious, of course, came in the 2006 Coupe du Monde final, when he became the first player to be sent off in the extra time of a World Cup.[14]

BEING, EVENT, AND THE PHILOSOPHY OF SPORT

*Most thought-provoking in our thought-provoking
time is that we are still not thinking.*
MARTIN HEIDEGGER, *WAS HEISST DENKEN?*

If you can keep your head when all about you
Are losing theirs and blaming it on you;
. . . .
If you can meet with Triumph and Disaster
And treat those two impostors just the same
RUDYARD KIPLING, "IF"

In thinking the events of Ron Artest, Eric Cantona, and Zinedine Zidane, *In Motion* has produced a structure of the event $(S_1–G–S_2)$ that reveals the event to be, like the rogue, idiomatically itself. The event is, in each instance, its own idiom and is true to the idiom out of which it emerges—the basketball court, race, racism, xenophobia, the secret, and so on. The event is everywhere, no more true of sport than in any other sphere of life and yet more intensely present, more rare and ubiquitous in sport than anywhere else; and yet the idiom of the event remains felicitously singular, recognizable only as itself. Thinking through and against transgression, through rareness and singularity, through movement, stillness, and *voyou*-ishness, through the idiom and intensity, *In Motion* makes it clear: provocation is what sport offers the event—a provocation that makes necessary, maybe even imperative, a new thinking of what happens intensely in the basketball arena, on and off the football field, across continents and cultures.

A new thinking emerges in this book primarily because *In Motion* tries to match the athlete and his event with the most appropriate philosopher, that is, the philosopher whose work thinks the specific event optimally. To this end, *In Motion* pairs philosopher and athlete, Artest and Badiou, Cantona and Deleuze, Zidane and Derrida, because each of these thinkers of the event, like every one of Artest, Cantona, and Zidane, has his own idiom of the event. These pairings are, as *In Motion* shows, hardly discrete—they inform each other, complement and complicate each other. And there are other philosophical figures, Heidegger most notably, whose work supplements this thinking. But there is, obviously, a certain primacy to the pairings. Badiou's strong notion of how the event radically changes things (in which his concept of supplementarity plays a key role) draws out the dramatic force of the Artest event; Deleuze's focus on the cinema, his ability to make history pithy, complements Cantona's propensity and preference for the enigmatic; and Derrida's work speaks to the issues, the difficulties, that surround the politics of the Other in republican France. In this regard, Derrida is closest to his athletic partner—both he and Zidane are, in their different ways, a generation or so removed, sons of the Maghreb who find their full articulation in France—one as a preeminent philosopher, the other as its greatest footballer (Raymond Kopa, of Polish extraction, and Michel Platini, with his Italian roots, are free to fight for second place). And Derrida, as we well know, was a keen footballer in his youth, so he and Zidane are perhaps best matched of all, because they share, albeit at very discrete levels, the idiom of football. Through *In Motion,* the sport's event finds a new use for theorists of the event.

Through these pairings, unlikely, strange, unthought of, and unimagined, *In Motion* has forged a structure that makes thinkable that which was already there but could only be made opaque, properly thinkable, because of the sport's event. The structure of the sport's event is such that, taken up philosophically, it makes it possible to know that which was already there but was not (yet) thought. Because of Artest–Badiou, Cantona–Deleuze, and Zidane–Derrida, that which was not known before is now, because of what happened in Detroit, London, and Berlin, eminently known. In this regard, we might say that the sports event is that intense articulation of the event that makes, in Badiou's terms, the truth known. The sport's event makes the truth of the event self-evident; approaching the sport's event philosophically reveals something of the underlying thinking of sport. This is a thinking that should be obvious but is only available when apprehended by, subjected to, philosophy: thinking the sport's event as event is what reveals the utter ubiquity of the event. It is possible to begin thinking for the event in sport. Sport can bring us to the event like no other event.

The effect of this recognition is, as *In Motion* shows, structural innovation—or is that renovation? *In Motion* insists: the events thought here demonstrate the event as it could only be made by, because of, sport. The effect of this cognition is important: it is a provocation of the Heideggerian order: "Most thought-provoking about our thought-provoking time is that we are still not thinking,"[1] that unforgettable refrain in *Was Heisst Denken?* Heidegger's answer is a firmly issued invitation that must be understood as a question: why are we still not thinking? Why have we not yet attended to thought? That is to say, Heidegger's question stands as a substantial challenge: "Everything thought-provoking *gives* us to think."[2] *In Motion*'s sport's event is given to thought to think about that which is not (yet) known about either the event or sport. Out of thinking Artest, Cantona, and Zidane, *In Motion* has crafted the sport's event—has crafted out of the sport's event—a structure for the event that turns on, as all three chapters demonstrate, a complex interplay between the poles of movement and stillness, between the idiom of the particular event and the idiom of the philosopher. *In Motion*'s is a structure made by action and inertia, given polarity by gnomic phrasings and articulately obdurate silences, a structure that arises out of the threat, the charm, and the ineluctable roguishness of the *voyou*—all elements that emanate and gravitate toward the pole that is the *voyou,* unquestionably one of *In Motion*'s primary and most alluring poles.

How does one resist the *voyou,* especially if he comes in the guise of a talented athlete who is also something of a rascal; if he can rebound with fierce determination, all the while throwing a surreptitious elbow in his opponent's direction; if he can score wonderful goals and admit to an affection for Mickey Rourke; if he can carry a nation's footballing hopes on his shoulders and, in victory or defeat, steadfastly keep his own counsel? What is Zidane, with his ability to treat all these "impostors just the same," if not a Kiplingesque figure? Not a one of them, not Artest, Cantona, nor Zidane, and Zidane especially, because his event belongs first and almost literally to the head, shows any ability to "keep his head." Salient, for the purpose of this project, is that they all know how to take themselves out of the situation. This does not, as we have seen, allow them to escape "blame"; on the contrary, it is largely, particularly in Artest's case, the reason that so much blame is heaped on them. Nevertheless, all three figures are committed to the art—the act—of subtraction because, in one way or another, they understand its power. So, in a paradoxical way, they can after all claim to have "kept their heads," their wits, about them.

They all come to rest because, at some level, in one (imperfectly understood) way or another, they grasp the utter signality of being at rest after being in motion—after being perpetually in motion, it seems. And because they know the power of being at rest, of stasis in a situation where motion is demanded, they are already—before the event—inclined toward the event, toward making it. As Derrida puts it, in a very different context, in *Monolingualism of the Other; or, The Prosthesis of Origin,* "they decided it all by themselves, in their heads; they must have been dreaming about it all along."[3] Artest (stillness) and Zidane (refusing, up to today, to reveal what it is he said) understand the importance of subtracting themselves from the action ("have they been dreaming about it all along?"; how long has the desire for subtraction lived in "their heads?"), from the event that they made, are in the process of making. They make the event through subtraction: it is a means of making the event that sport makes patent, makes forcefully visible.

Through his self-immobilization, Artest makes of the scorer's table a physically precarious (he is vulnerable to assault as he is lying there) but symbolically powerful political platform. Zidane provokes us to think, invites us to ponder, years later, futile though the undertaking may be, the power of subtracting into the secret, subtraction through the secret, the secret as subtraction. Few other figures of the political (the silent, still protester and political prisoner, steadfast in the face of violent repression, would be another such figure) harness the power of being at rest so effectively and dramatically. Cantona, a figure possessed of an elliptical stillness (his enigmatic tendencies punctuate, because of their rareness, his proclivity for speech), demonstrates his subtraction through his mastery of the gnomic. Faced with condemnation, he refuses explication, determined to play the poet (no doubt enjoying the role, too, thespian that he has always been), offering in its place the obscure and the abstract; his obscurantism and abstraction is a form of countering the demand for public explanation. Like Artest and Zidane, Cantona is a thought-provoking figure, not least because of his ability to deflect through inscrutable pronouncement.

But theirs is always an intense subtraction. Their predetermined, if we might borrow from Derrida for a moment, subtraction is an act that raises, makes visible, the philosophical (and political) stakes of subtracting the self. This subtraction possesses an intensity; it is by no means a passive act that is peculiar to the sport. Because theirs is an active at restness, their various subtractions lead, invariably, to intense reverberations. It is their subtractions that produce this singular intensity that flows from the playing field up into the stands (Cantona, Artest) or that breaches the playing field as it flows down from the stands (Artest, Cantona);

or the intensity is, a priori, ubiquitous, shared by all who come into the stadium, not least among them the players (Zidane and Materazzi). It follows, of course, that the greater the intensity of the event, the more pronounced and ubiquitous the reverberations. We must, then, be fully cognizant that the possibility for the event is ubiquitous—it is everywhere; the event is always expected to happen and yet takes everyone entirely by surprise when it announces itself. We are at once, such is our entirely understandable ambivalence (we might be mildly self-deluded too; after all, can we really be expected to treat these two "impostors" in the same fashion?), never sure that it will take place and never sure when the next event will take place.

However, as *In Motion* shows, there is one thing of which we can be certain. Whether we acknowledge it or not, we watch sport in anticipation of the event. We watch sport for the event; it matters not whether we enjoy the spectacle of the event or fear its capacity for disruption. And because this is how we watch sport, we are already watching sport as a singular provocation: to think the event. We have been "dreaming about it all along." Artest, Cantona, and Zidane have given us the opportunity to put our "heads" to the event.

ACKNOWLEDGMENTS

I could not have written this book without John Limon and Jeff Nealon. John and Jeff, each in his own inimitable way, made me, it often felt, go back to the beginning in order that I might start all over. Again. Both of them began with encouragement and then proceeded to make a list of demands that, it seemed, were absolutely necessary. They made me think about what I was trying to accomplish, they pointed out incompatibilities, they asked for explanations, they offered new ways to go about the project. They were invaluable to the writing of *In Motion, At Rest*. I owe them each, I am more than happy to say, an immense debt.

My Duke University colleagues, Michael Hardt, Orin Starn, and Ken Surin, were, as is their wont, generous with their time, supportive with their suggestions, and unfailingly kind. The first articulation of this project, especially the Ron Artest chapter, benefited from Orin's thoughtful enthusiasm and Ken's quiet urging. Michael was precise and encouraging in his reading of the Cantona chapter. I could not have written this book without their insights. And, as importantly, I admire the models of intellectual life they offer. All the faults, of course, are mine.

At Cornell University, Ellis Hanson impresses to no end as a scholar who not only values the intellectual project but does all he can to make it possible. This he does, mercifully, with a biting irony and a laconic sharpness, attired, always, with a coolness that speaks of immense self-possession. I am grateful to Molly Hite for her erudition and her deep sense of integrity. Few can match her courage and kindness. Riche Richardson is a colleague who subscribes to the primacy of thought. Most salient, however, might be her overwhelming decency. Debbie Fried is nothing short of a poetic delight.

Robert Caserio was an invaluable source of sanity and an astute reader, and a man insistent in his demand for that biretta.

Ian Balfour, writing, as always, from some trendy locale, offered a considered critique of the work after educating me about all the cool music to which I should be listening.

I owe particular thanks to Matthew Abraham and David Andrews. They showed themselves to be entirely considerate friends. I am grateful to Tom Lockwood and Debbie Stumpo for their immense kindness. Cary Nelson was acerbic, cutting, and funny when it mattered most. Joe and Denise were wonderfully supportive.

My editor, Richard Morrison, has been inordinately patient—in truth, far more patient than he had reason to be. His advice was measured and incisive. I have, over the years, come to rely on it.

My thanks to Eric Cazdyn (University of Toronto), Elspeth Probyn (University of Sydney, Australia), and David Faflik (South Dakota State) for their invitations to present earlier versions of this work.

My thanks to the editors at *Cultural Critique* and *Chimurenga*. Earlier versions of the Artest and Zidane chapters appeared in these journals. I am grateful to Ms. Milligan and Ms. Levine for their bureaucratic assistance. My thanks to my research assistant, Ms. Lee, for her self-possession; I could not have gotten everything ready in time without her. Thanks are also due to Lisl Hampton, who gave considered advice on the introduction.

For almost a decade now, first formally and then informally, I have relied on the editorial magnificence of Christi Stanforth. I admire your diligence, but not as much as I admire your calm. Thanks.

Juanita and I have reason, just about every day, to remark on how Nip is always a delight and a challenge, full of pithy and all-too-apropos phrases, possessed of a fertile and irascible imagination, brimming with confidence and eager to see the world (last spring's Barcelona mutates easily into this spring's Seattle into next spring's Paris). He is a constant joy in our lives. If only sleep would occupy more of his time.

My greatest debt is to Juanita. I admire her courage, her un-flinching honesty, the thoughtful way in which she undertakes her teaching, her commitment to cultural studies as a project that makes possible a deep and meaningful engagement with the world, her quite astounding parenting skills, her appreciation for the moment and the way in which she melds her politics and her writing. Gracias, mi amor.

This book is dedicated to my grandparents, Winnifred and Thomas Fisher. You always gave, whatever it was you had. You always gave without expectation—and with a humor that was gentle (Ma) and fiendishly mischievous (Pa). I think of you often.

Durham, Chicago, Ithaca

NOTES

INTRODUCTION

1 In this book, I use the term *football,* as the game is known all over the world, for what is commonly called "soccer" in the United States.

2 Alain Badiou, with Nicolas Truong, *In Praise of Love,* trans. Peter Bush (New York: New Press, 2012), 24.

3 Ibid., 78.

4 Jacques Derrida, *Rogues: Two Essays on Reason,* trans. Pascale-Anne Brault and Michael Naas (Stanford, Calif.: Stanford University Press, 2005), 87.

5 Ibid., 84. The full phrase reads, "the pure eventfulness of the event."

6 In *Rogues,* Derrida also raises the issue of "eventfulness of the event." Ibid., 87.

7 As we know from Derrida, nowhere is *différance* more evident than in literature.

8 Derrida names this phenomenon, pointedly and sardonically, as the "reason of the strongest," thereby ironizing the United States's invocation of "reason."

9 Derrida's two-year death penalty seminars that led up to the *etat voyou* work on this same logic.

10 The Pauline interrogative for this situation would be, of course, what radical revelation might the sport's event yield?

11 See Donald Harman Akenson, *Saint Saul: A Skeleton Key to the Historical Jesus* (Oxford: Oxford University Press, 2000).

1. RON ARTEST

1 In *The Kingdom and the Glory: For a Theological Genealogy of Economy and Government,* trans. Lorenzo Chiesa with Matteo

Mandarini (Stanford, Calif.: Stanford University Press, 2011), 250, Giorgio Agamben offers an archeology of "inoperativity." Agamben's archeology, which runs through a number of thinkers, from Aristotle (in relation to happiness) to Spinoza ("contemplation," 250; or how "inoperativity" is a prerequisite for thinking), is primarily interested in speculating—at this in his argument—how glory functions in contemporary politics. "Inoperativity" is useful, however, in thinking the body at rest because it touches on—in truth, it brings to the forefront—the place (and the precise political time) of stillness in politics. To be inoperative, Agamben shows, is not to withdraw from the political. On the contrary, to be inoperative is to create the time in which to take stock of how politics works, what makes it function (glory, for Agamben, is invaluable to any thinking of modern democracy; glory, so intimate with the *oikonomia* of the Trinitarian). Agamben's notion serves less as a counterpoint to, given the centrality of the Christian faith to Rosa Parks and the civil rights movements, than as a philosophical illumination of Artest's at restness. Agamben's notion makes yet one more gathering of at restness—inoperativity—possible.

2 This event provoked, as Stuart Hall might have it, a wide-ranging "moral crisis" in the media—a crisis about sport, about sportsmanship, about player salaries and their concomitant privileges, and about race, all of which produced, in a predictable convergence of these factors, an opportunistic attack on the culture of hip-hop and its influence on the NBA. See Stuart Hall, Charles Critcher, Tony Jefferson, John Clarke, and Brian Roberts, *Policing the Crisis: Mugging, the State, and Law and Order* (London: Macmillan, 1978).

3 Black interruption, and irruption, in this sense is reminiscent of Amiri Baraka's contemplations on black music. Baraka's argument is that bebop transformed (forced) segregation into a willful, productive, and innovative withdrawal from the mainstream. Bebop is what made jazz meaningful rather than just a form of victimhood. There would have been no Lester Young, Charlie Parker, or John Coltrane without a deliberate withdrawal from the vapidity of mainline American music. In sport, in music,

and, of course, in politics, black withdrawal—in itself, because of itself—constitutes a radical act that, in one way or another, transforms American life.

4   *Webster's Unabridged Dictionary,* s.v. "interlude."

5   The concept of the Situation is derived from Gilles Deleuze's notion of "SAS"—Situation Action Situation—in which Deleuze argues that the "situation is transformed via the intermediary of the action." Deleuze, *Cinema 1: The Movement-Image,* trans. Hugh Tomlinson and Barbara Habberjam (Minneapolis: University of Minnesota Press, 2003), 142. By itself, the Deleuzian situation is static: it must be activated, as it were, by the action which is itself not a situation. However, the Situation as it obtains in *In Motion* is itself an action: it is something that happens that might, say, inflame or instigate a Situation. The Situation is defined by the doing of something, by something having been done. The Situation contains within it the (potential) kernel of the event.

6   Martin Heidegger, "Building Dwelling Thinking," in *Poetry, Language, Thought,* trans. Albert Hofstadter (New York: Harper and Row, 1971), 153. Gathering, as Heidegger discusses it in relation to the ways in which the bridge draws the fourfold—earth, sky, divinities, and mortals—toward it, "expresses something that strictly speaking does not belong to it" (153).

7   Let me illustrate this with a comparison. A football player in a 2011 English Premier League game, Luis Suarez (Liverpool), says something to an opponent, Patrice Evra (Manchester United). What Suarez says, only for a moment, disrupts the flow of the game (because of Evra's response, which is captured on camera; later that same camera will reveal what Suarez had said). Well after the game has been completed, it emerges that Suarez uttered a racist invective against Evra. An inquiry is subsequently held by the English governing body, and Suarez is found guilty of racism and is fined and suspended (eight games). This is how the event (E) is the sum of the Situation$_1$ (original invective) that leads to the Gathering (inquiry) and another Situation$_2$ (fine and suspension). In Italy, in a friendly match between two teams from different divisions, AC Milan (Serie A; highest league) and Pro Patria (Leg Pro Seconda Divisione), fans of the lower league side

barrack a black Milan player, Kevin Prince-Boateng, with racist chants. Midway through the first half, Boateng picks up the ball and boots it into the crowd, bringing the game to a halt, and both sets of players leave the field in protest against the fans' chants. This is an event, pure and simple.

So, if the game is disrupted in its entirety because of a particular Situation and nothing else (Milan–Pro Patria), completely and radically interrupting the ways in which racism is confronted in football (Fédération Internationale de Football Association [FIFA] president Sepp Blatter condemns it as an inappropriate response to racism; previous pronouncements on racism by Union of European Football Associations president Michel Platini, asking for players who respond as Boateng did to be booked, are brought back into circulation; the Milan president—no less a personage than the former Italian prime minister Silvio Berlusconi—weighs in as to whether Boateng behaved correctly), then we have the event. However, if (Suarez–Evra) the original articulation does not, by itself, produce the event, then we have a Situation. Only when the Situation is Gathered (through the inquiry and the politics it generates), when it produces a certain discourse—about race, in this instance, though it could as easily be about, say, class or religion—that leads to the original Situation being Gathered into an other Situation, do we have the event. In such an instance, it is possible that the Gathering might not even know its own force as a Gathering in the moment that it gathers one Situation into an other; the Gathering might only come into its own, into its own language, in the supplementarity that engenders the subsequent (second or third) Situation. The effect of the Gathering is a further disruption, a series of acts or articulations that can (it is not inevitable) "elevate" the Situation into the event; the effect of the Gathering can always be traced, through the Gathering, to the original Situation. The Situation that "follows" (from) the Gathering is recognizable in that it not only amplifies the original Situation but intensifies and generates a whole new slew of meanings—interpretations, readings—because of the ways in which the original Situation has been Gathered. What Suarez first said, by itself, constituted only a Situation. Gathered, the Situation produced outrage from Evra and his club, and solidarity from Suarez's teammates (they considered him to have been misrepresented), nothing less than the event. The difference between what happened in Italy in 2013 and England a year or so earlier demonstrates that every event stands as the event but that the Situation will remain a Situation unless it is Gathered into an other Situation. For the Situation, everything depends on the Gathering.

The Boateng event demonstrates how we may, and frequently do, know the event by itself, but the Suarez–Evra event (S_1–G–S_2) enables us to grasp more fully the reach—the gathering potential—of the event. S_1–G–S_2 makes visible the historic power of the event. We know, insofar as it is possible to know, the event. What the formula makes possible is the capacity to attend to its constituent parts—it draws our attention, directs us toward, that which "makes" the event; the formula, provisional, imprecise as it is, allows us, prompts us, to think how to make it (more) knowable to us; it compels us to attend to the political and philosophical force of gathering. Gathering brings Situations together through its ability to, simultaneously, mediate and connect the Situations to each other, across the expanse of the Gathering, and in so doing it not only makes the event visible but renders distinct the larger stakes—race, gender, ethnicity, sexual orientation. However, as I make clear, S_1–G–S_2 is at best a partial explanation for the event—it is a formula that is helpful and, in moments, even incisive, but never exhaustive. The event must be thought, again and again, sometimes against itself. In this way, the real value of S_1–G–S_2 resides not in its scope, which is perforce limited, but in how the formula foregrounds the idiom of the event.

8 "A predominately white fan base," a *Kansas City Star* journalist wrote of the Palace Brawl, "is rejecting a predominately black style of play and sportsmanship." Jason Whitlock, "Black Players in Particular Should Heed Stern Warning," *Kansas City Star,* November 22, 2004. The media comments on the "thoughts" that predominated about the event—especially those denunciatory thoughts on the black male body, both inside and outside the NBA—revealed their conceptual limitations; the critiques

were unable to exceed condemnation or apologia, both of which are largely unsatisfactory. The project (or the imperative, we might say) is, for this reason, to read both the symptomatic and literal body of Ron Artest more "thoughtfully." How did the NBA go so rapidly from fan favorite to thug game? What, after all, has happened to the commercial cash cow that was, at least until Michael Jordan's initial retirement, America's most beloved sports spectacle? Did the "ghettoization" of the NBA, the rise of "His Airness's" heirs, the "bad boys" Allen (A.I.) Iverson, Latrell Sprewell, and, of course, Artest, happen overnight? Was the NBA not hip-hop before that? What was Dennis "the Worm" Rodman, him of the tattoos, the piercings, and the outrageous attire, teammate to Jordan, no mean acquirer of suspensions and hefty fines, if not the precursor—the single embodiment of a hip-hop black sensibility that was widespread during the Jordan era—to the generation of basketball stars who succeeded him? What was Ron Artest's number 91 Pacers jersey but an homage to "the Worm," who wore that same number during his tenure as a Chicago Bull? Or were Rodman's transgressions of a different order? More gender-bender, sexual provocateur, the embodiment of a cultural alterity at odds with the stereotypical heteromasculinist hip-hop aesthetic?

9   Walter Benjamin, "Theses on the Philosophy of History," in *Illuminations: Essays and Reflections,* ed. Hannah Arendt, trans. Harry Zohn (New York: Harcourt, Brace, and World, 1968), 261.

10 See my work on Ali and, to a lesser extent, on Johnson, in *What's My Name? Black Vernacular Intellectuals* (Minneapolis: University of Minnesota Press, 2003), for a fuller discussion on the ways in which these boxers subtracted themselves from—in their protest against—the American political.

11 Gilles Deleuze, *Difference and Repetition,* trans. Paul Patton (New York: Columbia University Press, 1994), 378.

12 Alain Badiou, *Deleuze: The Clamor of Being,* trans. Louise Burchill (Minneapolis: University of Minnesota Press, 2000), 8.

13 This was the case in, e.g., the 1989 World Series between the San Francisco Giants and the Oakland Athletics: an earthquake hit the Bay Area and delayed the World Series. This delay occurred

while the game was in progress. In a slightly different vein (because there were no games in progress), in the wake of the 9/11 attacks, baseball was suspended.

14 Badiou, *Deleuze,* 15.

15 Stephen J. Whitfield, *A Death in the Delta: The Story of Emmett Till* (Baltimore: Johns Hopkins University Press, 1988), 88.

16 The protest, conducted under the auspices of the Montgomery Improvement Association and the NAACP, was conceived by the latter organization's Women's Political Council wing, with key input from local activist E. D. Nixon.

17 Taylor Branch, *Parting the Waters: America in the King Years, 1954–63* (New York: Simon and Schuster, 1988), 128.

18 Ibid., 129.

19 Rosa Parks, with Jim Haskins, *Rosa Parks: My Story* (New York: Puffin Books, 1992), 1.

20 Badiou, *Deleuze,* 21.

21 In his series of lectures collected in *The Beast and the Sovereign: Volume 1,* trans. Geoffrey Bennington, ed. Michel Lisse, Marie-Louise Mallet, and Ginette Michaud (Chicago: University of Chicago Press, 2009), Jacques Derrida offers a necessary qualification to how Heidegger conceives the notion of gathering, a notion that serves as a caution against an unproblematic—a too easy—thinking of "gathering": "gathering is never, says Heidegger, a simple putting together, a simple accumulation, it is what it retains in a mutual belonging" (319). Following Derrida, it becomes imperative to account, at once, for the "mutual belonging" that Artest shares with Parks, Till, and Robinson and, as I argue, to refuse—if not refute, but certainly guard against—equivalencing their experiences. The event of Artest evokes the civil rights figures. There is no claim being made that he is equal with them.

22 Branch, *Parting the Waters,* 129.

23 Badiou, *Deleuze,* 35.

24 Ibid.

25 Alain Badiou, *Ethics: An Essay on the Understanding of Evil,* trans. Peter Hallward (London: Verso, 2001), 67.

26 Badiou, *Deleuze,* 91.

27 Martin Heidegger, *Was Heisst Denken?,* trans. J. Glenn Gray (New York: Harper, 1968), 16.

28 Branch, *Parting the Waters,* 141.

29 Badiou, *Deleuze,* 61.

30 Deleuze, *Cinema 1,* 142.

31 Deleuze names this the "acentered state of things." Ibid., 58.

32 Ibid., 11.

33 Ibid.

34 The system is in no way synonymous with the whole. The Deleuzian whole is replete with political prospect; its tendency is to open up, to make developments, relations, possible. The system bears the full weight of its repressive proclivities.

35 Badiou, *Ethics,* 67.

36 Ibid.

37 Before the event opens up into the whole, we are dealing with, in Deleuze's terms, the "set"—a finite number of objects, even though they can be rearranged; the set, however, is always for Deleuze a part—a subset, if you will—of the whole.

38 In the history of black athletes at rest, there is perhaps no more provocative a body than Muhammad Ali's. First, at his induction into the U.S. military to serve in Vietnam, Ali refused to step forward when his name was called, making him the most famous noninductee in American history; "I ain't got no quarrel with them Vietcong," he pronounced. And second, if more obscurely, in his fight with George Foreman for the heavyweight championship in Kinshasa, Zaire, Ali stood against the ropes and for seven rounds performed his "rope-a-dope" tactic, letting Foreman pummel him and, in the process, Foreman punched himself out; Ali won by a knockout in the eighth round. By standing against the ropes and absorbing Foreman's blows, Ali made a "dope" out of his opponent.

39 Cathy Caruth, *Unclaimed Experience: Trauma, Narrative, History* (Baltimore: Johns Hopkins University Press, 1996), 5.

40 Cabrini-Green was a public housing project constructed (by the Chicago Housing Authority) between 1942 and 1962 on Chicago's North Side. Originally a set of row houses (whose first inhabitants were mainly of Italian ancestry; it was, however, a fairly

integrated community whose members were employed, until the post–World War II factory closings radically changed their status), in subsequent decades, "Cabrini-Green" became the default moniker for the problems associated with public housing: gang violence, drugs, poorly maintained buildings, uncollected garbage, a minimally resourced community. At its peak, some fifteen thousand people lived in Cabrini-Green. By 2011, the last of the high-rise buildings had been demolished.

Artest grew up in the Queensbridge (built in 1939) housing project in Long Island City (in the New York City borough of Queens), the largest public housing facility in the United States. Queensbridge shares many of the same problems that marked life in Cabrini-Green—it is a dilapidated structure whose individual units are incredibly small, the buildings hardly attended to, rife with gangs and drugs.

41 Caruth, *Unclaimed Experience,* 27; emphasis original.
42 Terry Maxwell, "The NBA Brawl in Detroit Shows a Decline in Sportsmanship," *Arizona Range News,* December 1, 2004.
43 "Suspensions without Pay, Won't Be Staggered," ESPN.com news service, November 21, 2004.
44 Megan Manfull, "Artest Is the 1st to Be Suspended for a Whole Season after Brawling," *Houston Chronicle,* November 22, 2004.
45 Colin Twomey, "Turnin' Two," *Harvard Independent* 36, no. 18 (2004): 12.
46 King's language is, of course, much more poetic and memorable: "An injustice anywhere is a threat to justice everywhere." Martin Luther King, "Letter from a Birmingham Jail," http://mlk-kpp01 .stanford.edu. However, King's enunciation has a great deal in common, rhetorically, with Mamie Till Bradley's.
47 Whitfield, *A Death in the Delta,* 91.
48 See William Bradford Huie's contributions, originally published in *Look* magazine, on the combustible relationship among violence, race, the virulence of southern identity, and white (and black) poverty in Christopher Metress's collection *The Lynching of Emmett Till: A Documentary Narrative* (Charlottesville: University of Virginia Press, 2002).
49 W. H. Auden, "Concluding Lecture," in *Lectures on Shakespeare,*

ed. Arthur Kirsch (Princeton, N.J.: Princeton University Press, 2000), 312.

50 The fidelity of the event is such that it is worth remembering that there were no prospects of Artest-like renumeration available to Smith and Carlos when they returned to the United States after their defiant Black Power salute in Mexico City; for them, there was only rejection from the American body politic. Unlike Artest, who was able to resume his lucrative career in the 2005–6 season, the 1968 Olympians had no access to capitalism's marketing possibilities. While events may not happen only once, they certainly do not present the same economic prospects for all black bodies.

51 Badiou, *Ethics,* 70.

52 Ibid., 73.

2. ERIC CANTONA

1 Deleuze, *Cinema I,* ix.

2 Ibid.

3 D. N. Rodowick, *Gilles Deleuze's Time Machine* (Durham, N.C.: Duke University Press, 1997), 7.

4 Ibid.

5 In 2001 Cantona was voted the greatest United player ever.

6 Simon Gardiner, "The Law and Hate Speech," in *Fanatics! Power, Identity, and Fandom in Football,* ed. Adam Brown (London: Routledge, 1998), 250.

7 As quoted in Phillipe Auclair, *Cantona: The Rebel Who Would Be King* (London: Pan Books, 2009), 359.

8 Rob Wightman, *Eric Cantona* (London: Virgin Books, 2002), 139.

9 Auclair, *Cantona,* 359.

10 Eric Cantona, *The Complete Cantona,* with an appreciation by Tom Tyrrell (London: Headline, 1997), 14.

11 Eric Cantona, *Cantona: My Story* (London: Headline, 1993), 3.

12 One way players can extend or shorten the game is by exaggerating injuries ("faking" injuries, in the pejorative)—pretending to be more hurt than they really are to get the referee either to add more time to the game or to hasten the arrival of the end of the

game. These injuries tend to occur more frequently toward the end of games, when the outcome is at stake. In football, almost no one quibbles about time at the end of the first half.

13 Eric Cantona and Alex Fynn, *Cantona on Cantona* (London: Manchester United Books [André Deutsch], 1996), 20.

14 As quoted in Auclair, *Cantona,* 464.

15 Deleuze, *Cinema I,* x.

16 Michel Foucault, *"Society Must Be Defended": Lectures at the Collège de France 1975–1976,* trans. David Macey (New York: Picador, 1997), 6.

17 Ibid.

18 Auclair, *Cantona,* 355.

19 Ibid. The BNP and the NF are right-wing, xenophobic political movements.

20 Jacques Derrida, "Archive Fever: A Freudian Impression," *Diacritics* 25, no. 2 (1995): 10.

21 Ibid., 26, 27.

22 As quoted in Wightman, *Eric Cantona,* 142.

23 Ibid.

24 Cantona, *Cantona: My Story,* 105.

25 Cantona and Fynn, *Cantona on Cantona,* 14.

26 Ibid.

27 Terence Blacker and William Donaldson, *The Meaning of Cantona: Meditations on Life, Art and Perfectly Weighted Balls* (London: Mainstream, 1997), 50.

28 Ibid., 5.

29 Auclair, *Cantona,* 369.

30 Wightman, *Eric Cantona,* 141.

31 Ibid., 144.

32 Gardiner, "Law and Hate Speech," 250.

33 Ibid., 251.

34 Wightman, *Eric Cantona,* 142.

35 Derrida, "Archive Fever," 27; emphasis original.

36 Eric Cantona quoted on the Pride of Manchester website: http://www.prideofmanchester.com/sport/ericcantona-links.htm.

3. ZINEDINE ZIDANE

1 Mary Jacobus, "'Distressful Gift': Talking to the Dead," *South Atlantic Quarterly* 106, no. 2 (2007): 396; emphasis original.

2 "Thuram: 'If Mr. Le Pen Wants to Come, He Is Welcome,'" trans. Laurent DuBois, *L'Humanité,* June 30, 2006.

3 Zidane, who is by nature reticent, has taken a great deal of criticism from different constituencies in France—the Arab community, immigrant activists of various stripes, Muslims, and so on—for not using his status as national hero to speak out against discrimination against Muslims and Arabs and the mistreatment of immigrants. Here Zidane is often contrasted with two of his former national team colleagues, Lilian Thuram and Patrick Vieira, who are staunch and articulate advocates for the very causes Zidane has been asked to champion.

4 I am referring here to Derrida's explication of his relationship to his birthplace, Algeria, and the phrase that resonates so tellingly in that work: "I have only language, yet it is not mine." Derrida, *Monolingualism of the Other; or, The Prosthesis of Origin,* trans. Patrick Mensah (Stanford, Calif.: Stanford University Press, 1998), 3. Here Derrida gives his monolingualism a Heideggerian name, "dwelling," and constantly returns to his inability to "dwell" properly in this language that is not his. It is unclear whether Zidane struggles to dwell in France, in French, but he does seem adept at dwelling in what might be improperly named his propensity for silence, for keeping his thoughts to himself—his ability to dwell within himself.

5 The Heidegger essay invoked here is, of course, "Building Dwelling Thinking."

6 Derrida, *Rogues,* 159.

7 See "French Adore Zidane Headbutt Song," http://news.bbc.co.uk/2/hi/europe/5234062.stm.

8 "Materazzi Breaks Zidane Silence," http://news.bbc.co.uk/sport2/hi/football/internationals/5315618.stm.

9 There has been, in the last twenty years or so, a concerted effort by some of the game's authorities to stamp out this kind of behavior, from both players and fans. In England, especially, there has

long been a commitment to "kicking" racism out of the game; in Europe, where black players have historically been subjected to racial abuse, EUFA has targeted racism and other forms of attack. Furthermore, there has been a general commitment to what the authorities have labeled "respect," exhorting all involved in the game to treat players, fans, and administrators with greater regard.

10 Alice Kaplan, personal communication on *l'affaire Zizou,* October 2006.

11 Alec Hargreaves, *Multi-ethnic France: Immigration, Politics, Culture, and Society,* 2nd ed. (New York: Routledge, 2007), 90. See Hargreaves for a discussions of *Beur* as a neologism and, importantly, for tracing the history of the distinction between "Berbers" and "Beurs." See also Azouz Begag's *Ethnicity and Equality: France in the Balance,* trans. Alec G. Hargreaves (Lincoln, Nebr.: Bison Books, 2007), a text that offers an account of a Beur coming of age during the 1970s and 1980s.

12 Geoffrey Bennington in Jacques Derrida, *Jacques Derrida,* trans. Geoffrey Bennington (Chicago: University of Chicago Press, 1993), 71.

13 Jacques Derrida, *Mémoires: For Paul de Man,* ed. Avital Ronell and Eduardo Cadava, trans. Cecile Lindsay, Jonathan Culler, and Eduardo Cadava (New York: Columbia University Press, 1986), 229.

14 In the 1998 World Cup, during the opening-round match against Saudi Arabia, Zidane was dismissed for stomping on an opponent, the Saudi captain Fuad Amin. Together with the Cameroonian defender Rigoberto Song, Zidane is the only player to be given red cards in two World Cup finals.

EPILOGUE

1 Martin Heidegger, *What Is Called Thinking?,* trans. Fred D. Klieck and J. Glenn Gray (New York: Harper and Row, 1968), 45.

2 Heidegger, *Was Heisst Denken?,* 4.

3 Derrida, *Monolingualism of the Other,* 16. In this context, Derrida is discussing Vichy France's decision to disenfranchise Algerian Jews during the Nazi occupation. Algerian Jews had only "recently," in 1870, been enfranchised by the Decree of Crémieux.

INDEX

abuse, 73, 74, 102, 103
AC Milan, 157n7
Africa, 103; Maghreb, 146; North
   Africa, 118, 137
African American iconography, 45
African American life, 47
African American spiritual, 32
African American vernacular
   tradition, 36
Agamben, Giorgio, 156n1
Akenson, Donald Harman, 21
Alabama, 29, 42; law of, 43
Algerian Jews, 167n3
Ali, Muhammad, 16, 36, 162n38
America, 34, 36, 164n50; history
   of, 46, 63; life in, 47, 61; nation
   of, 52; in popular imaginary, 63;
   sport and, 35, 58
American football, 3
Amin, Fuad, 167n14
Anfield Stadium, 82, 103
Anglo-French antipathy, 14
Anthony, Carmelo, 60; Baltimore
   and, 59–60
Arabs, 97, 138, 166n3
archive, 102, 103
"archive fever," 102
Artest, Ron, 2–3, 5–6, 9–10,
   12–13, 15–20, 22–23, 25–37,
   40–41, 44–50, 52–63, 65, 67, 84,
   110, 142–43, 145–50, 164n30;
   Artest–Badiou, 147; Artestian
   body, 37, 55; Artestian clamor,
   37; Artestian moment, 67;
   Artestian principle, 49–50;
   Artestian Situation, 66; at rest,

27, 66; at restness, 6, 156n1,
   161n13, 163n40; Badiou and,
   146; body of, 20, 34, 61, 65, 148,
   149, 160n8; flagrant foul and,
   3, 5, 10, 25–26, 31, 34, 40, 52,
   55, 57, 60; Metta World Peace,
   5; NBA Championship and, 59;
   as NBA Defensive Player of the
   Year, 56; scorer's table and, 25;
   self-immobilization and, 149;
   St. John's University and, 59;
   stillness of, 148; when supine,
   20; time and, 32, 40
Asia, 103
athlete, the, 16, 23, 35, 48, 136,
   146, 148; black male, 33, 162n38;
   clock and, 79; distance and, 78;
   exceptionality of, 139; motion of,
   71, 74, 93, 98, 99, 100; NBA and
   the, 35; as philosopher, 146; as
   rascal, 148; as star, 16, 139–42;
   time of, 72, 98, 100, 101
at rest, being, 27–31, 34–37, 45,
   48, 49, 52–53, 59–60, 66, 112,
   142–43, 148–49; black bodies,
   27–30, 37, 162n38; body, 35, 57,
   58, 62, 64–65; restfulness, 56, 61;
   restlessness, 114, 116
Auden, W. H., 65
Auclair, Phillipe, 93
autoimmunity, 11, 18, 113
Badiou, Alain, 2, 3, 4, 20, 25–26,
   32, 37, 40, 48, 54, 57, 65–67,
   92, 146; Artest, Ron and, 146;
   Clamor of Being, 48; 1848 and,
   26; 1917 and, 26; *Ethics*, 48;

Grant Farred teaches at Cornell University. His books include *What's My Name? Black Vernacular Intellectuals* (Minnesota, 2003); *Long Distance Love: A Passion for Football*; and *Phantom Calls: Race and the Globalization of the NBA*. He was general editor of *South Atlantic Quarterly* from 2002 to 2010.